The

Teachings

of

Billionaire

Yen Tzu

21st
Century
Books

The Teachings of Billionaire Yen Tzu

Volume II

Published in Great Britain in 2004 by
21st Century Books UK Limited
30 Queen Square, Bristol, BS1 4ND
www.21stcenturybooks.uk.com
service@21stcenturybooks.uk.com

Cover Design by Dick Evry, Bath
Printed and bound in the UK by Antony Rowe Ltd,
Chippenham, Wilts

British Library Cataloguing in Publication
Data available

ISBN: 1-904956-01-7

The
Teachings
of
Billionaire

Yen Tzu

V
O
L
U
M
E

II

realising desires; needing nothing

Contents

Author's Note

There is a legend that tells of a famous Academy, now lost in the mountains of an Eastern Province. Founded some two and a half millennia ago by an immensely successful Patriarch, *Yen Tzu*, the School attracted the interest of great leaders, merchants, and individuals, from all over the ancient world; earnestly seeking the secrets of a new alchemy proven to deliver prosperity and well-being.

Possibly a member of the inner circle of Taoist Sages, *Yen Tzu* would have been fully versed in the Metaphysical Wisdom of the Ancients. His paradoxical philosophy, therefore, would have certainly followed the way of self-mastery through individual inner understanding.

Over several generations the School's acclaim grew through word of mouth, as each student, enlightened by their understanding of this new thinking, graduated. Such a level of understanding was certainly instrumental in *Yen Tzu* becoming Ancient China's first commercial billionaire; though such success inevitably attracted the attention of an aspiring Emperor.

History records that in the year 213BCE almost all remnants of this ancient teaching were destroyed by the first Emperor of what we now consider to be geographical China: the ruthless Qin Shi Huang, famous for the army of life-size Terracotta Warriors guarding his mausoleum; unearthed in Lintong County, Shaanxi.

Viewing such teaching as a threat to the divine rule he had decreed, he was convinced that by destroying it no-one would question or usurp his dictatorship. Pursuing this policy to control society's thinking, his brutal Prime Minister, Li Ssu, ordered countless sages to be executed and their places of learning to be burned to the ground. In an attempt to save them from destruction, valuable scrolls and texts were hidden in hollowed walls, a time-honoured custom utilised by numerous cultures over the ages.

History records that the Qin Dynasty lasted only during his lifetime, a mere forty-one years; a vivid reminder that motives seeking manipulation and control are always short-lived. Unwittingly, Qin had destroyed the very wisdom that could have been his greatest strength as a leader.

Yet, today, in the 21st Century and despite the immense power at our fingertips, the majority of businesses survive a few years and most people retire with little money. Clearly the application of a new thinking and practice is as valid now as it was to prosperity over two millennia ago.

Though there is growing awareness in the Western world of the danger of being enslaved to mindless consumption – indeed most of us prefer sustainable quality over disposable quantity – we continue to suffer on many counts. The labels of *me, my* and *mine* impose artificial limitations on the enjoyment of our life; and worrying over our status and what we can solicit from others prevents us from being true to ourselves.

There are many delusions to be cleared and the thought-provoking lessons taught by forgotten sages and harnessed by great leaders and merchants are revealed within this book. Although these revelations shake the pillars of current thinking, they uncannily strike deep chords within us, because of the sound truths that resonate from them. For achieving self-mastery through individual inner understanding is the only sure and timeless way to fully develop our potential, achieve our purpose and ensure our spiritual growth.

Paradoxically, through their initial obscurity, the answers currently sought by our modern world appear. Work can no longer be viewed as a separate compartment to the way we live our lives, either personally or professionally. With the increasing demand for a practical philosophy for meaningful, purposeful and sustainable success, my own research and hands-on studies led to me writing these two volumes. In doing so, I sought to unlock and share esoteric secrets and explain forgotten truths in the form of twelve lessons. They encapsulate through parables my interpretation of the genre of ancient wisdom, as taught by *Yen Tzu*.

By reading these volumes that comprise *The Teachings of Yen Tzu,* you will begin to perceive opportunities to test the potency of the ideas they contain. In this way you will become a graduate of self-mastery.

Colin Turner

Knowing the Eagle

Realising Desires; Needing Nothing

*H*ermit Wei glimpsed three eagles soaring above him. Calling them down to him he requested of the first: '*How much to carry me across the plains to the neighbouring state, please?*'

'*It's a two day flight at least and you are a heavy load,*' replied the first eagle, '*I would like ten fish, a goat and a flagon of soya milk.*'

'*So much,*' said Hermit Wei, and turning to the second eagle asked, '*What will you do it for?*'

'*It is right you are a heavy load,*' answered the second eagle, '*yet as I am due to go in that direction in any case, I would want five fish, a kid-goat and a flagon of rice-water. It is a long trip that will require sustenance.*'

Asking the third eagle what the charge would be, the hermit was surprised to hear: '*Five fish and a litre of water.*'

'*What kind of fool answer is that?*' Wei shouted. '*Why do you possibly ask for an amount that will not even sustain you for the trip?*'

'*I needed the order,*' said the crestfallen eagle.

'*Needed the order!*' the hermit returned angrily. '*Well my*

7

desire to go will not be at the mercy of your need. In compromising your worth you compromise my life! Come,' speaking to the second eagle, 'let us plan our trip. With your desire to go my way and your considered charge, I know my journey is assured.'

The Polarities of Desire

🗡 Healthy desire is the starting point of all achievement. The desire to live, for instance, is the unconscious motivation to take our first breath of life. There are, however, polarities to our desires, so that, depending on how much we want something, we can unwittingly bring about adverse conditions. A simple illustration of this can be seen by an ambitious individual, who desiring to impress others, brings about the opposite effect.

🗡 Our desires attract to us the elements which make us what we are and form our behaviour. The experiences we manifest in our lives, therefore, come from what we consciously or unconsciously attract to us. Every living thing displays a peculiarity because it has attracted a particular element to become so. The insect living in the mud displays different qualities to the insect living in the beautiful flower. The soaring eagle displays different qualities to the tiny sparrow. Man, who is the finished specimen of creation, reveals this doctrine in its fullness. His success and failures, his sorrows and joys, all depend on what he desires and what he has desired for himself. It is the nature of his intent behind those desires that counts.

✴ The question then arises: 'why would I want to desire elements which are undesirable to me, such as failure and sorrow?' The answer is that you did not desire them as you see them now, but as you saw them before. One does not seek pain purposely, one seeks pleasure, yet very often pain is hiding behind the facade of pleasure. Similarly a seeker of success may not see failure hiding behind what he or she believes to be success.

✴ Desires spawned from a false self lead to false activity and subsequent discomfort. One who desires a partner for the sake of parental pressure, appearance, security, jealousy, obsession, infatuation, habit or loneliness, will soon discover pain behind short-lived pleasure. Another who desires success for the sake of promotion, acquisition, status, title, money, respect or receiving the credit, will similarly experience a hollowness to their rewards.

✴ As the whole principle of creation is based on the power of intent, it is important to think and understand what you want and why you want it. When you enter into business with another, you must know the philosophy of your partner. When young people are in love, the intensity of their passion blinds their respective philosophies. With the short-term need satisfied, long-term limitations to deeper desires are overlooked. In complaining to ourselves that we never receive what we consider we are duly entitled to, there is no end to our complaining. Unconsciously we, in effect, desire something to complain about. Therefore, in order to have no complaints, we must become aware when and why we complain.

✝ In desiring things, we must distinguish, at each step in life, what we must manifest for ourselves and what we must not manifest for ourselves. Our lives are decided by our innermost pictures, generated by what we might wittingly, or unwittingly, desire from life. Fortune is not external; it is decided by how you desire it.

The Importance of Desire

✝ Desire is a form of energy linked to our lower physical and higher mental energies. Only when desire is out of balance with the higher energy functions of the mind, and serves the lower instead, does trouble follow. Out of physical desire, for example, a person may lose their calmness and clarity of mind and be compelled to act against their better judgement.

✝ The fact is, however, nature has designed desire and its proper use as one of the most important elements of life. Implanted in every living being is a strong desire for that which is necessary for well-being, nourishment and growth. Where perhaps spirituality gains release, for example, religion seeks control and, in censoring Man against the curses of having desires, has, metaphorically speaking, thrown the baby out with the bath water. Many of us counteract our desires with guilt, particularly in regard to relationships and wealth.

✝ The importance of desire is that with its power you already have the capacity to manifest, or attract, whatever you want in your life. The very fact you have a *desire*, the Latin root of which translates as 'of the father,' means that you have the God-given ability to achieve it. In other words you would be incapable of holding a desire unless you had the capability to create its reality. Although most of what we are taught to believe conflicts with this, your desires are the very tools that assist you in expressing your purpose. It is because of false indoctrination, however well-meaning, that the art of manifesting our desires for positive benefit has been forgotten.

The Four Keys to Higher Desire Power

✝ The Higher-Self is simply another title for the stronger, truer and real you, who, although never absent, is seldom paid attention to. When something just right for you arrives out of the blue, for instance, it is because your Higher-Self is acting in the interests of your honest desires. It is of course easier to believe that it is simply luck, coincidence, or 'too good to be true,' which is why opportunities are often ignored. Because your Higher Desire Power always operates indirectly, it causes you to take the longest way round as the quickest way for you to attain your desire. If necessary, therefore, it will cause your well-laid plans to be overturned, resulting in you thinking that failure and defeat, rather than success and victory, have come to you.

✤ Often it will have to tear you away from your existing, seemingly comfortable, circumstances, and throw you between a rock and a hard place in order to let you see the success it has attained for you. A characteristic of highly successful individuals is that they have experienced 'the dark night of the soul.' As one who has experienced finally ending up on the right track said: 'It took my whole world to cave in before I could see that the success I craved was beneath my feet. I was just walking in the shoes of someone I felt I should be, rather than wanted to be.' Although their previous false activities brought it on themselves, genuinely successful people always agree that the price paid was well worth it.

✤ It is usually because the four keys essential to channel your Higher Desire Power are never utilised that it is forced to take the action it does. How else can it realise your desires, which is its sole function, if you insist on building the frustration within you by virtue of being on the wrong track? Your Higher-Self freely employs the faculties of the subconscious and the collective conscious in its work to magnetically draw towards you what you ardently desire. It is not creating something for you; it is manifesting what already exists for you.

✤ Uninfluenced by the distractions Man fills his life with, homing pigeons, migrating birds, bees and animals lost over long distances successfully home in on what they want.

Anyone establishing a sanctuary for birds will tell you that even the strangest of species, indigenous to other countries, will soon begin to travel towards it. High or low, the Higher-Self will manifest its power. Man can harness Desire Power in the same way that he has successfully harnessed other great natural forces available to him, through application of the following four practices.

Accepting Your Worthiness to Receive

The brothers Po and Jo of Sung were inseparable as youths. Po dreamed of success as a merchant while Jo had resigned himself to the monastic tradition of his ancestors.

'Please do not enter commerce,' Jo entreated his brother, 'for the ways of business will make you unworthy to enter the Garden of The Jade Emperor and we will no longer be together.'

'It is not the ways of business that makes one unworthy, it is how much one allows one's self to be influenced by the needful habits of others. Anyway, learning to recognise such things may lead to the worthy cause of influencing others positively - who knows, I may run a state in time?'

'But you know as well as I do,' persisted Jo, 'that abundance and spirituality are incompatible. Both our elders and parents have always taught us to believe that it is both selfish and improper to visualise and desire success and material things. Already I fear that your ambition places you above your station.'

Six months after being persuaded by his brother's relentless admonitions to follow him, Po was talking to a visiting traveller.

'*I would have liked to enter commerce but it was an unworthy desire and realised it was only for selfish reasons,*' *said Po, in answer to a question posed by the traveller.*

'*Nonsense! When you deny your desire to follow a particular path,*' *said the traveller,* '*you deny yourself as the spiritual being you are. You cannot blame your brother's seemingly selfish action for making you feel unworthy about getting what you want and guilty for wanting it. Whatever you have, you allow yourself to have. Understand that what you really want matters, because that is what becomes matter. Material form is how the spirit of all things makes itself known to us. It is not selfish to want whatever you do in life and you should not be ashamed when what you want happens.*'

'*But it's too late. Everyone is content that I am a humble monk now. It is not worthy for me to receive what I once longed for.*'

'*It is true that what you receive is proportionate to what you believe you are worth, but never say that others made you into what you are today,*' *said the traveller.* '*Accept that you chose instead to acquiesce to the demands of others. From this moment say to yourself that you will be willing to accept full responsibility for whatever you bring into your life. Doing so will automatically place you in the position of becoming increasingly worthy to attract and receive whatever you desire.*'

Awaking, Po realised that there had been no traveller, he had simply been dreaming. Sharing his dream with the Patriarch of his brotherly Order, he was counselled to '*follow your heart's desire, for in so doing you become worthy of it and it becomes worthy of you. Everyone's path is different, yet only a few ever recognise the integrity of a true desire, and in doubting it cause themselves to become unworthy to receive it.*'

Following his dream Po became a successful trader and, in time, his worth was recognised by Duke Mu of Ch'in, who made him his high minister.

❡ Too often we allow the conditioned beliefs and admonitions of others who have low self-regard, to exert influence and power over us. In doing so we put on the clothes that validate the unworthiness that for so long has adorned them. Thinking that success and riches are incompatible with spirituality, for example, is one of the largest contributors to feeling unworthy.

❡ It is a sad fact that the amount of self-worth a child feels reduces dramatically during its formative years. Whenever children are able to resist the consistent hypnosis of being limited in their abilities, they are able to express their unlimited selves and manifest the abundance and opportunity they want throughout their lives. But it is, of course, impossible for most children to resist the ideas and limiting beliefs of their surrounding influences. Adhering to a curriculum of teaching to get by in life, rather than get on in life, the emphasis, unwittingly, is on reducing self-worth, and thereby limiting the child's potential rather than releasing it. Most teachers and parents will freely admit that although they recognise that praise develops growth, the emphasis is on correcting mistakes.

❡ It is therefore vital, as adults, to accept personal responsibility for redeveloping our worthiness to receive.

This means acknowledging that our self-esteem comes from ourselves, not from others; accepting ourselves without complaint and refusing guilt into our lives.

✯ Anything that promises worthwhile results is easier said than done, but, as personal development programmes are almost non-existent both at school, where we spend a good part of life learning, and in the work environment, where we spend a much greater part, it is up to every individual to be accountable to themselves.

✯ Being accountable involves taking ownership as well as responsibility over your own growth. It is acknowledging that empowerment does not come from others, because you can only empower yourself. When you know that only you are responsible for how you choose to react to every life situation and stop blaming others, your shift in consciousness increases your worthiness to receive.

✯ To accept yourself does not mean to accept every conditioned behaviour, which can be altered, but it does mean to stop mentally chastising yourself and putting yourself down. Self-repudiation is in disharmony with your Higher-Self, as are persistent feelings of guilt that prevent you from manifesting anything worthwhile, and instead attract to you the very same things about which you are sending out messages. Such things, when received, frustratingly provide yet further rationalised evidence that you are not worth what you desire.

✝ In refusing to allow former conditioning to dictate the limits of what you deserve in your life, you automatically allow yourself to accept the abundance and opportunity that is available for you.

Applying Your 'Rightness' for Receiving

Yuan Wen was a merchant of jade. His business was to take intricate and beautiful adornments to the houses of people who liked to buy. One day he was sharing his business psychology with his friend, Yen Tzu.

'In the trade of jade there is great scope for dishonesty, yet every day I am further convinced of a spiritual truth while doing my business. Most days I take my gems for people to see, I honestly tell them the right price and mostly I see that they are sold, and profit by it.

'However, it is hard to always be a saint in business. Sometimes I have felt that a customer is really attracted to an item and, sensing his want, I have added a little more to the price. In doing so, it seems that I was robbed of some power, and experienced a sense of loss during the day. This is no coincidence, for not just once but many times this has happened. It seems that whenever that temptation robbed that sacred power within me, then that day I was not successful in my business.'

'I too will admit to this experience in past times,' said Yen Tzu to his friend. 'What does this show us? It shows us that hidden within our heart is a Divine Power that is able to be

developed by keeping what we attract to ourselves in harmony with what we want. Whenever we allow need, greed or speed to influence our desires, they are distorted and come back to us with a sense of emptiness. This in turn leads to a change in our attitude and behaviour which others sense and either reflect back to us or cause them to become suspicious and disinterested.'

✱ The degree to which your three areas of thinking, feeling and behaving are not in harmony is in direct proportion to your ability to attract what you really want. This means examining the attitudes that you knowingly, and sometimes unknowingly, hold about your life.

✱ Your attitudes are expressions of the way you think, the very frames of reference you have constructed to support your world. It follows that if matter is thought made concrete, then your thoughts are the architects of your material world, and your attitudes the builders. If you have thoughts about how you want to conduct your life and then behave in a manner that does not reflect this 'rightness,' ultimately you become self-defeating in your ability to manifest.

✱ Life is full of temptations to test our 'rightness' attitude. Our tendency is to constantly complain about our conditions. Yet, if we were immediately placed in the conditions we so desired, rather than feel satisfaction we would soon feel the scarcity in those conditions also. This is because we seek to only fulfil our outer needs, which do not satisfy the emptiness within us. The question arises, therefore, of how can we become in harmony with the conditions of life when they conflict with our desires.

✌ Those who complain most about life and who are the most disappointed and troubled will inevitably struggle the most, whatever their conditions. Such complaining reduces our ability to apply our rightness to receive. A condition as bitter as poison can be turned into nectar by getting in rhythm with it, and this can only be done with a rightness of attitude. When experiencing a period of favourable conditions, a person will fear for the time it will end, and will even ask, 'Yes, but how long will it last?' Yet, when experiencing an adverse period they do not think of when it will end, rather they wallow and complain about it and announce 'Oh dear, what is to become of us.' This is illustrated by the fact that bad news travels faster along the grape vine than good news.

✌ The very nature of life, from morning through to evening, is that everything changes, so why should we not believe that bad times will change and good ones will come? In allowing ourselves to fall into the habit of expecting the worst, we directly affect our attitudes and desires. In doing so we generate fear and agitation which only serve to get us further out of rhythm with our condition.

✌ Many imaginative and intelligent people who read every little struggle in the daily newspapers allow themselves to believe that the world is falling to pieces. Others, whose own world is currently in pieces will exclaim, 'What am I to do?'

And if their world is not in pieces, then some will conclude that 'it will be harder to survive in the future.' A few will not concern themselves as they forge ahead, despite the ups and downs going on around them, while, at the other end of the scale, extremists will conclude that astronomical signs, such as an approaching comet, portend the end of the world and end their own lives.

✝ When your attitudes and desires are misguided, because you have the opportunity to get away with something, or because you rationalise that a particular difficult condition warrants such an attitude, your ability to receive is distorted. By ensuring that your attitudes and desires are right you become in rhythm with your Higher Desire Power. Consequently you are guided to that which is right for you regardless of the conditions that life presents.

Developing Prosperity Consciousness

Four merchants met on the road to Tai Kwok Market. After initial pleasantries they began to ask each other why prosperity shone on some and not others.

'It is wealth that makes life run smoothly,' said the first. 'Yet despite my good efforts I never have any, and I am continually fraught. So, for my part, I am certain that to receive prosperity, you must first have wealth.'

'Having wealth is not the difficulty,' said the second, 'it is keeping it that I find so hard. The more I try to hang on to my

wealth, the more it seems to diminish. So, for my part I am certain that to have prosperity, you must first keep it.'

'Keeping wealth is not the difficulty,' said the third, 'it is the making more of it, while keeping what you have, that I find so hard. Despite making more it never seems to provide me with enough. So, for my part, I am certain that to keep prosperity, you must first make it.'

'Having, keeping or making wealth is of no consequence to receiving prosperity,' said the fourth, 'it is whether your thinking is one of abundance or one of need. So, for my part, I am certain that it is not your purse that makes you rich or poor. It is your thinking, and it is only abundant thinking that will cause prosperity to shine upon you.'

✦ Generally when people don't have, they think about not having; when they have, they think about how to not lose it; and when they keep it safe they think about how there is never enough. Therefore, people who are worried about not having enough allow it to infect their consciousness so much that they merely endorse the insecurity that denies prosperity.

✦ Those who need things are at the mercy of a scarcity mentality. Most people, as well as the majority of businesses, suffer from this, although they are unaware of it. Often seemingly successful in spite of themselves, their competitive outlook actually limits them. The need of an individual for a greater income is no different from the need of a company for greater turnover and profits. After all, the actions that run a business are the expressed thoughts of the individuals that fuel it.

¥ Consistent growth and increasing profits are, of course, a healthy benchmark of business. Indeed, without profit there can be no business. But the 'need' outlook takes the view that when a slice of the market pie is taken, there is less of the pie to enjoy. The rarer 'abundant' outlook takes an entirely different view. For example, just because one person is fluent in a language does not mean that another cannot learn, for there is plenty of vocabulary for everyone.

¥ If you think poor you will stay poor, because your thinking is focused on what is not wanted. Ask anyone what they want in a relationship, in business or in life, and it soon reveals how they view their world. When they say: 'Let me tell you about what I *don't* want in a relationship' or 'I know what I *don't* like about business,' then you can be fairly certain that they are suffering from a scarcity consciousness, and will normally believe they never have enough.

¥ Developing an 'abundant' outlook means not having to think about your needs. It means establishing your wants and thinking only about those. Thinking abundantly is accepting that there is a natural course to obtaining what you want. It will require effort, but not struggle. Whenever you experience yourself struggling with something, be assured that it is not for you. Moreover, if you continue to struggle you are putting yourself in the world of the needy. On the other hand, healthy effort, however fervent, which leaves you feeling that what you are doing is worthwhile and important, is definitely for you. It is vital that these alternatives are recognised, as the former means you are operating from a scarcity mentality, whereas the latter confirms you are operating from an abundance mentality.

𝑌 Dependent on your thinking is your propensity to attract or repel prosperity. To develop a wealth consciousness is to never again think about what you lack, and about what others lack, and to never view the success of another as confirmation of your lack of luck. Rather, whenever you hear news of a friend, relative or colleague who has done well, use their success as confirmation that there is infinite abundance for you also.

𝑌 Begin to accept, both intellectually and emotionally, that any scarcity thinking has both originated and developed, either consciously or unconsciously, from listening and being influenced by others. Then allow your thinking to accept, both intellectually and emotionally, the image of abundance in your life as being perfectly natural. Doing this over just a few days will make you aware as to how your shift in thinking will alter your expectations. This, in turn, leads us to the most important of the four practices.

Letting Go of What You Want

'At last,' Tung Kuo said to himself, 'with this latest commission how splendidly I will be able to live!' In orchestrating the

negotiations for Master Tien to take over the Ch'ien Low business of Yueh he had excelled himself. All the work was done and he simply had to wait. In six months the Registrar of Yueh would ratify the deal with the Ruler's Seal.

As the time went by all he could think about day and night was how he would be able to fulfil all his desires. There were many luxuries he had decided on, he could settle all his debts and, more significantly, his status among his peers would rise.

'Why do you not work these past five months?' colleagues would ask. 'Has the deal you live for come off already?'

'It will any day now so my time is fully taken up in getting ready for when it does.' replied Tung Kuo excitedly.

Why couldn't his family be so excited? he thought to himself. His uncle had advised against becoming so attached to a future event — could he not realise how important this was?

'But it is the security I have been desiring for so long,' he had argued.

'Your desire for security is good, but it will not come from attention to the future, it comes from attention to the present,' his uncle had replied. 'Beware of attaching your emotional energy to something in the future or you will become like a prisoner bound with the chains of anticipation. You have sent your desires out, now detach yourself from their outcome or the price of freedom may be costly to you.'

Rather than let go Tung Kuo tied himself up in emotional knots as the time when he would hear news of the deal's conclusion drew nearer. He became increasingly impatient and irritated with everyone he spoke to and had no time to think about anything else. Family, colleagues and creditors getting on with their own daily functions, kept out of his way.

Receiving a letter from Master Tien close to the appointed day, he excitedly tore it open. The message was to inform him that due to the sudden assassination of their Ruler by the men of Yueh, it was not possible for the registrar to ratify the sale of Ch'ien Low's estate. Indeed, the letter added, both the Registrar and Seal had been removed from office.

Tung Kuo never fully recovered from the stroke that he had instantly suffered on reading the letter. It was some time later that his family were able to inform him about the further news received the very same day. Master Tien had omitted to say in his first letter that as both Ch'ien Low and he still wanted to proceed, albeit recognising it would have to be much later, he would still pay commission. An alliance had been agreed with a much lower price so, whenever Tung Kuo wished to present himself at The House of Tien, he would receive payment.

✢ Whenever you are about to say something and a distraction in the conversation causes you to forget whatever it was, experience tells you that the act of forgetting it brings it back. What you want to impart to another may be on the tip of your tongue, but the more you refuse to let it go, the more elusive it becomes. It is the act of letting go that allows you to recall it. If it comes to you much later, rather than earlier, it is because it took you longer to relinquish it.

✢ It comes to you because your attention is occupied with something that is relevant to the present moment, such as driving. As long as your attention is in the present, then your intent for the future will manifest itself. The real power behind fulfilling a desire is your intention, because intent is desire without attachment to the outcome.

✙ In creating a garden you would not consider pulling up recently planted flower seeds to see if they are growing, yet the tendency with the seeds of desire is to become emotionally attached to them. In doing so you are centering your attention on a specific result in the future. In order to manifest whatever it is you want in your life, you have to be able to let go of your emotional attachment to the outcome.

✙ This is a metaphysical ordinance. Holding on to things disturbs the manifesting of your desire, so that even if what you want comes through, it will be distorted. This is because there are infinite possibilities available in the way in which your un-manifest desire can be expressed as a manifest reality. This uncertainty allows your desire, sent out by your intent, to return to you in a form that may even exceed your expectations.

✙ The level of energy and rate of vibration that the desire created by your intent emits, will seek correlation with the vibration that matches the desire and bring it to you. Your detachment from any outcome accelerates the natural process of creation, whereas your attachment to it freezes your desire, impeding the fluidity of your intent's vibration, thus breaking the process.

✙ Springing from poverty consciousness, attachment is based on the fixed belief that security will be gained through external symbols that validate the individual desiring them. Material goals and objectives that are worthwhile and bring benefit to us are a healthy part of personal development and a positive measure to monitor growth, but they must never be viewed as providing the security that people constantly seek. The fact is that the search for security outside of ourselves will always elude us, and at the best remain short-lived. Attachment to money, for example, will always create insecurity regardless of the amount.

⚥ Getting wound up because you feel the need to attain certain symbols, whether in the form of titles, status or money, makes you the slave of your desires rather than the master of them. Think about what it is you currently desire. The level of your emotional attachment to its outcome will be indicated by how frustrated you feel by it not happening yet, and how much you feel compelled to force, or think about forcing, a solution.

⚥ Detachment, on the other hand, is born of a wealth consciousness, because, when what you desire has no hold on you, you are free to create whatever you want. One of the best examples of realised desire and detachment is allowing the child, you've nurtured to the best of your ability, under your earnest intent for their well-being and happiness, to go to live their own life without feeling any impediment from your emotional attachment and judgement of them. The major reason for conflict within families is when emotional attachment, expressed via control, becomes the form of security.

✤ Similarly, one of the major reasons for conflict both in individuals and business is the forcing of solutions in order to fulfil a need. It is easy to see that the scenario of desiring to exceed all expectations in the way you perform, harnesses your power. Yet the opposing scenario of needing something at all costs, which compromises your power, usually predominates.

✤ Your desire to improve your lifestyle either by wanting a better car, promotion or more business, for example, indicates your innate power to be able to bring it into your life. But an emotional attachment to whatever it is you desire will immediately and significantly diminish this power and allow all manner of debilitating emotions to gnaw away at you.

✤ Letting go of an outcome does not require you to compromise your values or objectives and, moreover, will ultimately bring to you what you want. Not letting go, however, will cause you to incur force and stress that will compromise more than your outcome; you will compromise your health.

The great eagle, its huge wings covering its craggy mountain eyrie, was not immediately aware of losing one of her young as she tried to protect them from the fierce storm. The mother hen in the farm below was similarly unaware that something had dropped into the soft hay of her coup.

Reared to behave as a chicken, the young eagle never learned to fly; completely unaware that his nature was to be a king among birds. A passing hermit noticed him awkwardly holding his great wings while strutting and pecking with the other chickens.

'Don't you know what you are?' said the hermit, gently taking the eagle in his arms. 'Your nature is to soar high in the sky. Come, stretch forth your wings and fly.'

The hermit's action confused the eagle, however, and as he did not know who he was he jumped down to rejoin the chickens. For several days the hermit persisted, each time taking the eagle to higher ground, saying: 'Know that although you may live like a chicken, inside you beats the heart of an eagle, a great eagle, know that you are the king of birds. Go, stretch forth your wings and fly.' But each time, the eagle appeared unaware of his true, unknown, self, and awkwardly hopped back to join the chickens who were scratching for corn in the dust. The hermit noticed, though, how the eagle would cast a few glances at the sky, almost as if sensing something stir deep within its heart.

Finally the hermit carried the bird to the top of the mountain. Reaching a steep crag far above the chicken coup, the hermit held the bird aloft while repeating his words of encouragement. 'Out there, among the heavens is where you belong. Go now! Stretch forth your wings and fly! Become the eagle that you are.'

But still the bird did not accept its true power. Not knowing what to do the eagle's powerful vision swept back and forth from his coup to the sky. He could see the chickens pecking at their food, and felt that he needed to be back there. Then, as if spying something far in the distance, he began to tremble and *slowly stretched out his wings. It seemed to the hermit that the eagle was growing in stature and, just at the moment when he could no longer hold him, the great eagle let out a triumphant cry and soared into the heavens.*

🦅 In letting go of what it had been conditioned to need, the eagle was able to gain its heart's desire, although attachment to what it considered its security to be prevented it from immediately knowing this. None of us were born to scratch out our needs in the dust. Yet, in forgetting our true identity, many of us cede our immense power for realising our desires in favour of the needs that circumstances and conditioning dictate for our security.

🦅 Accepting our worthiness and applying our rightness to receive whatever we desire, means knowing what we want and why it is we want it. Developing our prosperity consciousness as to how we receive, and having the courage to let go of our emotional attachment to whether we receive, means acknowledging the power of our true selves.

🦅 Like the great eagle, we can desire everything, whilst needing nothing. It is the ability to let go of what you think you need that gives you the power to realise your desires.

Fighting the Rat

Harnessing Conscience Power

'What a terrible dream I experienced last night!' howled Gate-Keeper Yin to his wife. 'A giant rat would not desist from chasing after me until, finally, with no place to turn, it had me cornered.'

'Heaven protect us against such things! What did you do?' his spouse enquired earnestly.

'What could I do but attack it,' Yin continued. 'And I fought hard let me tell you, but in the end I was sorely wounded. But then a very strange thing happened. Just as I lay in a defeated crumpled heap of humiliation, expecting the final mortal blow, the rat spoke to me. It said: "You win," and immediately helped me up, which is when I awoke. What awful misfortune can it possibly foretell?'

'My old mother was wise,' answered his wife seemingly calmer in her remembrance of something. 'She would say: "When you have a fight with your conscience and get beaten, you win!" Maybe that rat was your conscience and you've gone and cornered yourself.'

'How so?' asked Gate-Keeper Yin, and his thoughts immediately flew to his actions of the past week. With so many people arriving for the festival this year, he had allowed his greed to get the better of him. He had charged more, in the certainty that, with so many travellers, he would not get caught out. Some had looked perplexed at the toll cost, a few had made him feel a cheat, but as most had simply paid up, he had ignored the feeling which then soon left him. Anyway, he reasoned, he deserved such perks!

'Don't ask me, I am no sage!' replied his wife. 'Though I would imagine that any battle you lose with your conscience must mean you ultimately win. Particularly if it causes you to stop doing something that will bring you no good. Have you been up to no good?'

✔ Conscience is that part of our consciousness that is vital to our development and growth. However, there is conscience and *true*-conscience. The former is subjective, the latter objective. We often think the function of our subjective, or *conditioned*, conscience, is to spoil life for those of us who are unlucky enough to be pricked by it. It could be said that, 'your conscience doesn't keep you from doing anything; it merely keeps you from enjoying it.' In this guise it can be likened to an irritating acquaintance that you have periodically to tolerate. All too often we construct an entire framework of intelligent rationa-lies-ations in our attempts to justify actions that contradict our deepest sense of right and wrong.

✔ Without understanding and development of our true-conscience, that internal guide that provides clarity and guidance, its valuable power will remain untapped. It will lie dormant behind our conditioned conscience which asks: 'Will I be found out?' If not we reason, then everything will be okay. When true-conscience is harnessed, however, we are able to break down the internal barriers that prevent us from facing our inner contradictions and see the truth about ourselves. In doing so we are able to achieve a level of inner security that is reflected in every area of our personal and professional lives.

✯ There are numerous situations that although seemingly small and insignificant, we see as a normal and acceptable part of our everyday behaviour, both personally and, in particular, professionally. They will often appear as simply the *normal* way of doing business in the world. We cheat on our taxes or expense account; we tell little white lies in our business dealings; we keep quiet when we are given too much change. Though we like to believe that our word is our bond, we change our minds about honouring agreements that we have made with others, hiding behind a man-made caveat. We exaggerate or omit information as we consider appropriate, in order to get what we want.

✯ Conscience guides us as to what is good or bad concerning our conduct with others. Yet we have become adept in generating a rationalisation for every one of our small dishonest acts, in order to justify them on a mental level. On a deeper level, however, as they remain unjustified and unresolved, they drain our sense of self-worth. Over time their amalgamated and compounded effect contribute to confusion, guilt, loneliness, ulcers, cancer and heart attacks, as our inner fears and conflicts attack our bodies.

Culture, Morality and Conscience

❡ A difficulty in discriminating between our conditioned disempowering conscience and our true empowering conscience, is that what is seemingly right for one particular culture may be viewed as wrong by another. For example, one culture may choose to receive payment from the person accused of causing the death of a family member as appropriate compensation, but this custom of accepting 'blood-money' could be considered immoral by another culture. Because of different cultural views, therefore, it is also important to differentiate between morality and conscience.

❡ Very simply, where morality is relative, always different and always changing, conscience is absolute and never changes. Morality can be both subjective and objective. Take the example of cheating another, objectively accepted as wrong by Mankind, but too often subjectively acceptable between people of different classes, education and even countries.

❡ Conditioned conscience comes from an association of ideas. Such an association can cause us to act in a particular way in order for us to feel comfortable about what we do. Although there may indeed exist, or have existed, those rare individuals who actually appear to be without conscience and do what they do for the sake of evil, the purpose of the conscience is to direct for the good. A person acting from conscience may cause destruction in the misguided belief that they are doing so in the interests of good, and this in itself illustrates the havoc a conditioned conscience can cause.

Although history records various atrocities perpetrated by seemingly remorseless individuals, it also records that, without exception, what they unconscionably strove to create eventually crumbled.

✗ External morality is different everywhere, as exemplified in the maxim: 'When in Rome do as the Romans do.' For inner morality you must be able to do; that is do what you know to be true in the very depths of your heart. When developed to its stronger and deeper state, your true-conscience becomes a powerful guiding tool of perception and direction.

✗ People will always claim that if it weren't for your conscience, you'd probably do everything you want to do right away. In educating our conscience, however, we are able to align what we do with what we are. It also helps us to recognise that there are universal principles, independent of us, allowing us to understand the futility of trying to become a law unto ourselves.

Keys to Releasing Conscience Power

✗ Dealing with others, who do not appear to have a conscience can often create a rationale for not heeding our own. The truth is that as long as your conscience is your friend, you never have to worry about your enemies. However, the thought of responding differently from a habitual fear-based reaction may appear so frightening that it is almost unimaginable to us.

✤ Could we really confront our boss or client? Could we really tell the truth or say what we think, even if it meant that the outcome was not the most financially desirable? Could we really live true to our conscience, even if it meant being fired or impeding our advancement? Could we really trust that we would be peacefully guided towards our next job, contract or opportunity, instead of remaining in a compromising situation or fearfully grasping at whatever becomes available to us? Whatever fears we feel corner us, it is not until we confront them that we will stop feeling compromised in a way that literally drains our energy and potential.

✤ In harnessing our conscience we will be clearly guided towards balanced growth and development. There are three specific keys which when practised will release the power of true-conscience, allowing it to become the ally and trusted advisor it is intended to be.

Motives over Moves

T'ien K'ai was a rich philanthropist whom everyone in the village liked. Whenever he himself received further good fortune he would share it by giving rice and money to the poor. One very poor man received a heavy sack of rice which he happily took home to his family. Upon emptying it into his storage bin, however, he discovered ten gold coins mixed in with the rice. His wife was delighted but the husband said, 'Lord T'ien K'ai gave me rice. He did not intend for me to have this gold. I must make him aware of his mistake by returning the gold to him.'

'Don't be such a fool!' His wife said. 'We are poor and he certainly won't miss a few coins as he has immense wealth. Give them to me and I will go to the market and change them for money.'

They argued but the husband was adamant. 'We must not be greedy. I cannot take what is not intended for me. Anyway, it was I who brought the rice and the gold home in the first place.'

Returning to T'ien K'ai the following day he told him, 'You were so generous in giving me and my family such a large sack of food, but I have discovered these ten gold coins. I've come to return them as, although I am a beggar, I am not a scoundrel and can recognise a mistake when I see one.'

The rich philanthropist was moved by the poor man's sincerity and replied, 'I want you to keep them, and because of your sincerity, I will double their amount. You came with ten coins and you will leave with twenty and I give these to you now, personally, so that you will know there is no mistake.'

A greedy merchant happened to overhear the story and he came up with a brilliant idea. He visited the poor man and offered to exchange six of the gold coins for money. The poor man was happy to oblige. Then, putting on the clothes of a beggar, he went to visit the house of T'ien K'ai.

'I will do the same thing as the beggar and double my wealth,' he said to himself. 'With the hundreds of bags that have been received by beggars I will never be suspected as not being one of them.'

When his turn came for an audience with T'ien K'ai the disguised beggar said: 'Yesterday you gave me three coins but look! They have magically become six coins today. I have, *therefore, returned to your house so that I can give back the original ones to you while I am keeping the other three.'*

'Although one man brought back the same amount that I gave him,' replied T'ien K'ai, 'you are the only person to whom I have given, whose wealth has increased. I am delighted for you, but tell me, what can I do for you now?'

'It is said that you value honesty,' answered the merchant-beggar. 'If, because I am returning your coins, you are impressed with my honesty then, perhaps you will reward me with more. After all you would never have known the original three produced three more if I had not returned.'

'Yes,' said the philanthropist, 'you do deserve more. But since you have already made six from three coins let me give you something much more important than just a few more.'

'What reward to you have in mind?' enquired the excited merchant curiously.

T'ien K'ai summoned his first secretary and instructed him to write out a Certificate of Honesty. When it was completed T'ien K'ai attached it to the false beggar's back and signed it. 'There you are,' he told the merchant-beggar, 'This certificate will announce to the whole world that you are a most honest man. I have never awarded such an honesty document to anyone else. But you deserve it.'

✔ The only way to keep the goodwill and high-esteem of the people we work and live with is to deserve it. Each of us will eventually be recognised for what we are because of our motives, not for what we try to be through our moves. Having the right motives will always win over making the right moves, yet, often prompted by personal ambition, we focus on gaining quick success by learning artful techniques. In the long run, no techniques, no matter how clever, can conceal the motives a person has in his or her heart.

✯ Many businesses focus on making all the right moves with the understandable motivation of greater return. Indeed, the majority of employment training is on specific competency techniques to ensure that the right moves are practised. But the motives behind practising the right moves are not always in harmony with what the business pertains to be in business for.

✯ Take two competing pharmaceutical organisations, for example. Both giants in their industry, committed to providing essential cures for the greater enjoyment of life. One company may seek to maximise its returns so that it can invest into further research and development in order to keep its pipeline of essential cures flowing. Another may seek to maximise its returns so that it can bring greater return for its shareholders. The first considers that developing new cures is its life-blood and this is in line with its motives. The second considers that its shareholders goodwill is its life-blood.

✯ Both companies are making the right moves. Yet do they both have the right motives? Without further development, what will the second company do for new products? It will need to effect the take-over of another pharmaceutical company in order to obtain further products. This may be the right move, but the consequential reduction of duplicated personnel will inevitably mean the disappearance of many people, ideas and research that would have led to new products.

❧ At the other end of scale are two small businesses. Both are specialists in their industry committed to providing greater efficiency in the operations of their clients. The first, seeks to sell its products and services in the belief that they will make a difference. As such this company is discerning and does not seek to sell its products if it believes they are inappropriate for the customer's requirements. This is in line with its motives. The other, however, is motivated to sell because its over-extended budget must be met. Regardless as to whether a product is appropriate or not, it believes that so long as the right moves are adhered to, success is assured. It is essential to focus on the right motives as then the right moves naturally follow.

❧ To receive rewards with financial or career success by making the right moves, at the cost of high self-esteem and peace of mind, is to have sacrificed something of real value for trinkets. When we exchange gold for trinkets, the quantity we amass is irrelevant. Initially, and for a limited period, possessing the trinkets may be exhilarating, but you will not keep people from noticing the difference.

❧ Walk into the building that houses any business that you are not involved with and you can soon tell whether its moves are consistent with its motives. Hidden agendas, dichotomy of values and duplicity of motives that have become 'the way it is around here' cannot be concealed for long from an outsider. The tension generated by inconsistent motives can permeate a whole company.

✔ Notice, for example, the tension we experience when trying to please people from whom we want something. As an individual you only have to ask yourself if you feel differently talking to someone that you want something from, than you do when talking to someone that you don't want anything from. When you are sure of your motives you believe in what you do and why you are doing it; then you can learn to become as relaxed with others as you are when by yourself. Questioning your motives on a regular basis will automatically develop the power of your true-conscience. In doing this your conscience helps you to be sincere with yourself.

✔ When we are unsure of our own motives, it follows that we will be unsure of the motives of others. Understanding the motives of others accurately, however, would clearly be an immensely valuable tool as all areas of our lives involve interaction with others. Understanding of the right motives is infinitely more important than simply acting out the right moves, and this leads to the application of the second key.

Facing the Fear of Honesty

'But, father, how can I tell the teacher? Everyone will say that I ratted on Li-Li and hate me!'

Yu Kan looked at the despair in his son's eyes and his heart went out to him, while his mind recalled how his own schooldays had taught him to face the grim realities of battling with a misguided code of honour. 'You must ask yourself, how you cannot,' he replied. 'This is no simple prank. If you saw that it was Li-Li who was the real culprit and say nothing, then everyone will have to take the blame.'

'Yes, but everyone is prepared to,' his son argued, adding quietly, 'because they are scared if they do not. Li-Li has said that if anyone tells then they are a coward and, as such, they will deserve to be punished, by him.'

'Yet, each time he gets away with his behaviour he seems to grow worse, from what you tell me. With everyone's silence clearly condoning his actions, no-one is helping him to question them.' Yu Kan paused. 'You must follow what your conscience tells you, for to know what is right and not to do it is as bad as doing the wrong yourself. It takes greater courage to do something that you feel you should do, than to not. The coward is the one who does nothing, when everything inside directs them to do something.'

'But why me!' said his son looking horrified at what his father was implying. 'Why do I have to do anything? Why can't someone else?'

'Because only you can fight your own battles, and your own battles are the ones you feel strong enough about. The pain that you imagine lies ahead of you for doing the right thing, will not be as great as the pain you will give to yourself for not doing so. You will not like yourself.' Again Yu Kan paused. 'So, there is your choice.'

'So, either I hate myself if I keep quiet, or, everyone hates me if I speak out. Some choice!' answered his son.

'That's it,' said Yu Kan. 'But remember real honour and respect comes from being your own man, not from being fearful of the whims of others.'

The following day the boy went to Li-Li and asked him to own up to what he had done. Li-Li refused and threatened a beating if the boy was to tell. The boy did tell, and the next day he sported his bruises proudly and, after a short time, became more popular than Li-Li, but for all the right reasons. After all, he had confronted and conquered his fear of being dishonest. He liked himself and he could live with himself. He was his own man.

¥ The moral and ethical situations that we encounter in both our personal and professional lives are important opportunities for us to choose between fear and its opposite, love. Having the courage of your convictions stems from how much you like yourself. Before continuing, reflect on the following. On a percentage scale of one to one hundred, how much do you like yourself?

¥ Identifying our fears is usually the easiest part; it is confronting them that is difficult. If we peel back the layers of our fears far enough, we will often discover that their main source lies in our belief that we feel we are not worthy or lovable. A form of 'honour amongst thieves' leads to misguidedly believing that 'ratting' on the wrong actions of another is a crime. Speaking up for yourself is not about collaboration with the enemy. Tribal associations of 'not telling tales,' follow us from school through to social and work dilemmas. In allowing the creation of such fears we directly affect our own self worth. Indeed, the majority of abuses, physical, emotional or mental, remain unknown, or continue, because of prior conditioning to keep quiet about them.

✯ Acceptance of intimidation at work, for example, can be observed everyday. An unanswered email to a subordinate will be perceived by a 'bully' as acquiescence while, in truth, the recipient believes his or her silence indicates their non-acceptance. Internal e-mail permits blanket bullying of whole departments that stay silent, reserving their complaining for unofficial lines of communication in the canteen or at home. Tapping into a grapevine shouts louder than official lines, yet, remains unheeded.

✯ As our fears have often been with us a long time, we come to believe that we are not worthy of the respect, success, financial stability and peace of mind that we really would like. We perceive situations in a fearful way, based on indoctrinated beliefs such as the following:

1. Sometimes you have to do things that are not entirely ethical because it is part and parcel of career advancement.
2. Looking the other way is sometimes necessary to achieve success.
3. Everyone does it, so if I don't do it as well then someone else will beat me to my goal.
4. Business is business and its ethics are different from my personal ethics.
5. It is not going to hurt anyone and it's not illegal, so why not do it?

6. If others do not see through my deceptions then it's more fool them.

✔ Most of the major situations that we have to face involving ethical dilemmas will be created by, and thus correspond to, our dominant fears. The greater the fear, the more intense the situation will appear, with major ramifications for those involved; our keeping quiet, or not telling the truth, may effect someone's job, reputation, or feelings. We may be asked to lie in order to prevent a large sum of money being otherwise lost and which in turn would mean us not receiving the promotion or contract that we had hoped for. It may be that we simply do not take the responsibility to resolve the harm our mistakes have made.

✔ It is usually our fears which govern the codes that are deemed part and parcel of success in business: we fear that if we respond differently to everyone else, we will not be liked, accepted, or asked to be involved. We fear that if we appear to be a threat to the status quo we will be passed over when it comes to promotion. We fear that we will fail if we follow a course of action that is compatible with our sense of business ethics. We fear that confrontation, or encountering the disapproval of another, will threaten our job security, future contract or income.

✔ Whatever our fears, until we confront them with our own sense of honesty, we will not release them and they will continue to plague us. We can be hurt by nothing; the hurt we feel stems from interpreting our dilemmas as proof that our fears are indeed valid. If we fail at something, or incur disapproval, we consider this to be outright proof that we are unworthy, incompetent, not good enough and unlovable. When we confront someone and incur their anger, we think this is proof that we must be wrong and they must be right. In truth, this is not proof that any of our fears are valid, only that we allow them to exist in our mind.

Confront and Conquer

✝ Overcoming our fears means that any dilemmas that may arise in our lives disappear, as situations are perceived differently. Once again what in truth is simple is often difficult to accept. The situations that each of us create by our fears should be viewed as blessings, each with a role to play. All bring us the same opportunity to learn to release our fears and allow confidence to emerge in their place.

✝ Each time you confront and conquer your fears you are allowing your true-conscience to grow in influence. In doing so you avoid failures and, indeed, view any setbacks as valuable lessons when encountered. People with high self-esteem and no fears about their own worth are excellent people to work for and with.

✝ As we release our fears, the confrontations that had previously caused us pain become fewer, and the disapproval from others that made us feel so rejected becomes acceptable. This happens in direct proportion to our realisation that we cannot, and should not, try to please anyone by compromising our sense of worth and developing values. There is actually no such thing as a tense or uncomfortable situation with others. What has really bothered you is the behaviour and explanations you think you owe to others. You owe nothing to others except to be real, for you alone can give true value to yourself.

✴ Trying to impress another, looking for approval, hanging onto someone's every word, expressing contrived concern for another's well-being, explaining yourself, are all examples of you compromising your honesty with yourself. This is done in the false belief that you are strengthening your position with others. Being honest with yourself means never having to explain or complain.

✴ By reminding yourself of the invalidity of your fears, as well as the benefits gained each time they are conquered, you will actually start to anticipate eagerly, rather than dread, those situations that allow you to confront them. Each time you confront your fear of being honest with yourself, you may still experience its reappearance. But its hold over you will be weaker and it will no longer be the dictator it was previously. It will simply be an emotion that you are aware of, but it can no longer influence you to discontinue the path that you know is right.

✴ You will discover that you no longer use financial or career criteria as the dominant determinant in your decision making. You will trust that if a deal does not happen or is lost, a better one is waiting on the path ahead of you. This path may appear painful at first, as it could appear as a loss of something. But this sacrifice is an illusion, as any path that is grounded in integrity and balance will not only take you where you want to go, but provide peace of mind and fulfilment along the way. This path follows in union with application of the third key.

Non-Justification of the 'I'

'Yao Kou, you promised last week that you would be here on time.' Tan Lee said to his partner. 'Yet, you let me down again.'

'How so?' the astonished partner replied. 'Me, late? Well, I may not always be punctual, but I am never late! Anyway, it is not my fault. I had every intention of getting up earlier this morning but, upon awaking, I noticed it was raining so I decided to wait awhile before leaving, as the market road would probably be awash. As it turned out it wasn't, so I am able to be here now as I said I would be, though I can't remember promising.'

'It is said that if you find it difficult to be sincere with yourself,' Tan Lee returned, 'it is not possible to be sincere with others.'

'Your trouble is that you always speak in riddles,' replied Yao Kou. 'What has sincerity got to do with it? It is simply that sometimes I find that the "I" that declares that it will rise early in the morning is different from the "I" that exists in the morning, who refuses to co-operate. Having so many different parts of him must be why a man, for instance, finds it so hard to keep something secret. First one "I" makes a promise, believing that he wants to keep the secret. Then, tomorrow another "I" in him prompts him to tell his friend over a bottle of rice wine. With a different "I" in command, a clever person may question a man in such a way that he himself is unaware of what he is saying.'

'You're not trying to say that you have revealed what we discussed together last week are you?' enquired Tan Lee. 'We agreed that would remain between ourselves only for the moment.'

'I met with the trader Fu'li, we drank and I couldn't help it. But I can't say I'm sorry because it has been worth it. Fu'li raised doubts which I believe we should seriously consider. Anyway, it's hardly my fault. You should have made it clearer or at least given me all the facts.'

'I could not have made it clearer,' said Tan Lee. 'Yet, listening to you reminds me of the teachings of that great sage who visited us from the west: "If one of thine 'I's' offends thee, pluck it out." For without unity in your thinking you will continue to justify your own actions through blaming other people or things. It is clear that my "I" met with your wrong "I" last week, so, all of me tells me I must depart. Goodbye.'

✢ The New Testament reminds us that *If thine 'I' be single thy whole body shall be full of light.* In other words, only the true unified self is able to reveal its pure potential. A disunited self remains limited. This follows the holistic principle that the sum of the parts is greater than the Whole when brought together. When we are not in unity we will always seek to justify our actions. Yet by learning non-justification we are able to develop greater unity within ourselves. This in turn, allows greater confidence.

✗ The conditioned mind, formed by restrictive and limited thinking, does not want its false sense of security threatened by any unified thinking. So to prevent you from fully knowing yourself, it develops numerous *'I's'* and divides them into thought-proof walled compartments; we compartmentalise what is effectively the same emotional feeling about something. At one moment we feel one thing and at another something quite different. Each time you think 'I will do this'; this is later overridden by another *'I'* occupying a different compartment that chooses to do something else. This *'I'* in turn, has no dominion over the next *'I'* resting in a further compartment.

✗ Man, in his conditioned state, is a multiplicity of *I's*. Likening the unified self to a dollar, then every moment you say 'I' you use a cent. Although we think we see the whole of something, we actually only allow ourselves to see a part because of the walled compartments we insist on putting everything into. Opinions and prejudices are examples of solid walls which we allow to become permanent through fixed ideas and misconceptions about ourselves. In turn, opinions and agendas, depending on the compartment, become chameleon-like, created to suit a particular situation or role.

✔ Unaware of their own agenda people can believe that 'they may not be always right, but they are never wrong.' Learning to become aware of our tendencies to label or pigeon-hole everything and everyone we meet, allows us to develop greater flexibility in our thinking, while trusting in our developing conscience.

✔ Each of us experiences many different roles in life which make up our Whole 'I'. Each one of the 'I's' delegates its duty to another, which in turn does not recognise the authority of the previous. Each separate 'I' is able to act, however, in the name of the Whole, to agree or disagree, to give promises and to make decisions with which another 'I' will have to deal. This explains why people so often make promises to themselves and so seldom carry them out.

✔ The 'I' who decides to take time to consider what is really important in your life promises to start that very evening. The evening 'I' will take another view, however. This one will consider that the subject of your personal evaluation is far too important for you to do now, so chooses to defer the task until the week-end. In turn the week-end 'I' to which the task has been delegated has other plans. After all, how can you spend a well-deserved break doing something so important? This 'I' easily delegates to the future 'I' that will be in command on your holiday. It is no concern to the new 'I' what has been decided previously when it takes office, as former 'I' governments have no jurisdiction.

Raising consciousness

An Eastern allegory compares Man to a house full of servants whose master and head steward are absent. As the servants forget their roles and do what they like, with no co-ordination, the house ends up in complete chaos. The only possibility for things to improve is for a number of servants to agree to appoint a deputy steward. The elected steward can then command the other servants to do the right work in the right place. There is then every possibility of the head steward returning to replace the deputy and to prepare the house for the master's return. The master can be likened to your true-self, which can only appear when the level of consciousness of knowing who you are has been attained. As the unified true-self once more takes command from your disunited conditioned self, you no longer feel the need to compartmentalise everything to fit previous preconceptions.

⨪ This is a level of consciousness that does not seek justification for any of your actions. Being in a unified state of mind allows you to follow the counsel of your own heart and live the life you're intended to live by making your own decisions, rather than passively submitting to what others think is best for you. This will involve putting yourself first, which of course runs contrary to what we have been taught.

⨪ The truth is that to be sincere with others we must first develop sincerity in ourselves. There can be no other choice, in the area of personal development, than to put ourselves first. This does not mean running roughshod over others; it involves consciously accepting that only you have the power to make yourself either happy, or unhappy. In making yourself happy you are able to create happiness for others because your increased self-esteem does not need to justify itself. Only when you have made sense of yourself can you then make sense of the surrounding world.

✤ Becoming conscious of our habitual tendency to be judgmental towards others, or to seek justification for our own actions, allows us to tune into our true-conscience. This allows us to have a bird's eye view of all our different compartments and reveal to us how we really feel about something.

✤ Being aware of those times when we feel we have to justify ourselves provides us with the opportunity to dissolve a false 'I' and instead listen to the guiding voice of a surer, developed conscience.

The Winning Corner

✤ At one time or another, everyone feels that they have been a rat. Whenever we have behaved badly, particularly in relationships, we put it down, in all honesty, to our acting out of character. 'I can't believe I said that!' we exclaim, or 'Was that person really me?', or 'I just wasn't myself.' Our conscience seems to work best whenever we are being observed by another. How much better it is if we can begin to observe ourselves as another might.

✗ Harnessing our true conscience through:
- fully understanding our motives, before making a move;
- being honest with ourselves as to what is really important to us, so that we are not prepared to compromise regardless of persuasion;
- not feeling that we have to justify our actions, because we have the confidence that they have been initiated by a more unified self,

provides the power that will unerringly guide us towards balanced growth and development.

✗ Our ultimate goal is for peace of mind. Everything that is meant for us and our highest good, be it a job, promotion, a relationship, or sum of money; and every action that leads us to what is right for us, will come from listening to our true-conscience. Whatever *dis*comfort we experience will derive from our behaviour based on false fears.

✗ Whenever circumstances demand a compromise from you, take the opportunity to re-examine your motives to resolve any fears you may have. If you feel you have to compromise your true conscience, accept it as an indication that you need to alter your circumstances, perhaps leave a relationship.

✗ Beware of looking for the angle in everything, as in doing so you place yourself in uncomfortably tight corners, and drain yourself of energy in fighting to get out. But remember, though one of the most painful wounds in the world is a stab of conscience, it is good that you always win, because it may otherwise disfigure the soul.

LESSON

9

Seeing the Snake

Raising Awareness and Concentration

*S*everal people were walking along the north road to Han Tan early one morning when they each came in turn upon a man lying in the roadside. The first person, pausing in his journey, said out loud, 'That man must be drunk and sleeping it off, probably after gambling all night at the Mah Jong House I'll wager. The scoundrel ought to know when he's had enough and go home, rather than sleeping where it suits him!' Continuing on his way he shouted, 'The gutter is the best place for you.'

A second passer-by said worriedly to himself, 'He could be dead having been bitten by a poisonous snake. There are some venomous ones in these parts I hear.' Hurrying ahead he soon overtook the first man.

'Poor unfortunate,' thought a third person, a little later, 'He must be very ill and looks as though he doesn't want to be disturbed. I better let him rest where he is.'

A fourth man following soon after, thought, 'That must be a travelling holy man, one who is above ordinary physical consciousness. What austere clothes he wears and a strange stick he has. And that net sacking that surrounds him appears most *uncomfortable. But then such a saintly man can meditate anywhere, be it a ditch or a temple, sitting or lying. I must be careful not to disturb him.' And bowing, he too carried on.*

Meanwhile, the first man had caught up with the second, who had previously passed him. The first had not spoken to the second earlier because he had felt the man was not worth talking to. 'What's that scoundrel hiding, hurrying like that,' he remembered thinking. The second man was motioning for silence with one hand to his lips while pointing with the other to something half on the road and half hidden in the undercover. 'Look there,' he whispered. 'It's a snake, just as I thought. And by the look of its orange and black markings it is lethal.'

'It looks more like a bit of coloured binding rope to me,' the first man said. 'There are many merchants passing here and that's been dumped there by some scoundrel I expect.'

'Still, to be on the safe side,' said the second, 'let us together throw a heavy rock and trap whatever it is.'

It was half an hour before the other walkers discovered to their horror the remains of two badly mauled bodies lying in the road. Both had seemingly died in a bloody instant. While desperately wondering what dreadful fate had befallen the unfortunates, they were soon joined by the same man they had seen lying in the road side earlier.

'Am I too late?' the newcomer shouted breathlessly. 'Did any of you see which way the beast went?'

'Beast, what beast?' shouted the others in terror. 'Quickly tell us what devil is living in these parts?'

'It is no devil,' replied the man. 'It is the mascot of Chao. I am Third Keeper Mo Kop, protector of General Li Mu's leopard.

The Cat Beast is a treasured gift that escaped two days ago and I, among others, have pursued it without rest. Until last night that is, when, desperate for rest from my exhaustion, I must have collapsed at the side of this road. Now I'm ravenous. Have you any food?'

'Food! How can you think of food! What about these unfortunates? And what are you doing letting such a beast out in civilised parts? This is Sung Province, not Chao. What right has one of your Generals got to bring death here?'

'The same right that you have to travel to Han Tan, capital of Chao,' answered Mo Kop, flatly. 'And as for these poor devils, well, they must have chanced upon the leopard while it too was asleep, though for it to set upon them is strange. It must have thought they were attacking it, for it has never reacted before in this way.'

Third Keeper Mo Kop scratched his head in consternation. 'Oh dear, I can see already that if the mascot is in any way hurt I will be made to pay dearly! Oh woe am I, and it was not even my fault the beast escaped. Still,' he added, brightening up as he ran off, 'by my ancestors, at least it is not First and Second Keeper lying here, as I first thought. Perhaps with good fortune they are at this moment recapturing our mascot!'

✷ The world, as each of us perceives it, is nothing but our own projection. We see what we expect to see because the way we perceive is based on our individual frame of reference, formed by our conditioning, through which we interpret everything we experience. And what we perceive has to fit, for if not, we just don't see it. People will always see what they have decided to see, construing their world according to how it should be, rather than how it is.

✠ The scoundrel, therefore, sees a scoundrel; the drinker sees a drunk; the worrier sees problems; the saint bows to a saint. Yet all are mistaken. Where one sees what his frame of reference perceives to be a snake, another sees something dumped by a scoundrel, yet both are unaware that it is really the tail of a dangerous animal. If heaven and hell are states of consciousness we allow ourselves to occupy, then if there is hell in your mind, you won't see heaven anywhere. If there is heaven in your mind, you can't see hell.

✠ Because of our fixed frames of reference, our tendency is to *pre*judge, or have prejudice against, anything that does not fit our expectations. Our perceptions distort our beliefs, our values, our commitments and our communications with others. Unaware that they may be inaccurate we react with cynicism or are sceptical when confronted with anything that lies outside our frame of reference.

✠ Too often the refrain of: 'If only I had been aware of that', has escaped the lips of either the hasty person, who causes unnecessary stress or anguish by jumping to conclusions; or the immovable person, who overlooks opportunity through their refusing flexibility. All misunderstandings and missed opportunities spring from our inaccurate perceptions, yet it doesn't have to be that way.

✯ Waking up to the fact that we are blinkered is the first step in gaining awareness. It often takes a shock of some kind for this to happen. Whatever the shock, be it personal or professional, there is always a positive side effect should we choose to use it to gain greater awareness. In reaching a higher level of awareness we gain significant rewards and are able to achieve much more while expending less energy.

✯ Too often we tend to continue to get the same results, because we continue to do those things that we have always unconsciously done. In other words, if we carry on doing what we've always done, we'll carry on getting what we've always got. The alternative, being consciously aware of whatever we do, brings greater achievement for less effort; it is not the hours you put in that count, it is what you put into the hours. Or, put another way, one insight will resolve a thousand difficulties.

✯ Being aware gives you the ability to develop open concentration. Lack of concentration is the cause of most accidents, so the ability to concentrate is fundamental to survival. But open concentration is far and above ordinary concentration. It is the ability to bring focused attention to what you are involved with, while remaining conscious of what is happening around you.

✯ Many people believe that meditation, a growing practice in the West, is a form of concentration. Any meditation, however, that leads you deep into concentration makes you

more and more closed rather than open. Whenever you
narrow down your consciousness you become unmindful of
the surrounding world. Where the scientist, for instance,
becomes absent-minded because he is concentrating on his
problem in hand, the great sage is not a man of closed
concentration; he is a man of awareness. In being unaware,
the scientist may hit on the point but miss the greater
picture. Concentration makes you single-focused at great cost
– all other aspects of life are ignored. Open concentration
takes everything in and is thus infinitely more effective.

✯ Concentration involves focusing the mind on form;
contemplation involves focusing of mind on an idea; meditation
involves raising consciousness. Working in harmony the three
are able to create a state of relaxed intensity which allows clear
perception, creativity and focused attention to come together.

✯ This heightened awareness will naturally allow you to
focus on what you know is clearly the right direction, while
creatively harnessing all the opportunities and situations that
you accurately perceive around you. Application and practice
of certain keys are fundamental to assisting you in reaching
this state.

Observing Self-Evaluation

*'I would be honoured to assist your Greatness in this matter,'
said Chih-Po, rushing forward.*

Counsellor Tang turned in the direction of his approaching assistant and asked, 'Are you aware of the difficulties associated with such a business as this?'

'Listening to you, your Worship, has provided me with the knowledge associated with such a business as this,' answered the bowing courtier. 'You just have to instruct me on the outcome that you want and I will see that it will be done.'

'Even if what I might want may cause rifts for the people or business concerned?' questioned Tang.

'Although a humble assistant counsellor, my lord, I am a teacher, and as such believe myself to be a good judge of character. I do not have to meet the men to whom you refer, to be of the opinion that, as they have brought such consternation to one so revered, their actions must be in question. As such, any injury that I or another may give to them is simply their due brought on by themselves.'

'Well, I know these men involved and I believe them to be good, which is why I am questioning my own thinking.' Counsellor Tang commented.

'Of course, your Honour,' replied Chih-Po. 'Allow me to visit them in going about their business so that I can report to you...'

'Enough!' interrupted Counsellor Tang. 'How can you evaluate others when you yourself possess the Eight Faults and apply the Four Evils that beset the undertakings of all men.' And turning to the advisor on his right said, 'Chang, remind this "judge of character" that anyone knowing themselves must examine each one carefully.'

'Yes Counsellor,' replied Chang who, turning to face Chih-Po, proceeded to do so.

'To do what is not your business to do is called officiousness.

'To rush forward when your comments are unsolicited is obsequiousness.

'To echo a man's opinions and try to draw him out in speech is called sycophancy.

'To speak without regard for what is right or wrong is called flattery.

'To delight in talking about other men's failings is called calumny.

'To break up friendships and set kinsfolk at odds is called maliciousness.

'To praise falsely and hypocritically so as to cause injury and evil to others is called wickedness.

'Without thought for right or wrong, to try and steal a glimpse of the other party's wishes, is called treachery.

'These eight faults inflict chaos on others and injury on the possessor.

'As for the four evils,' continued Chang, 'these are:

'To be fond of plunging into great undertakings to enhance your merit and fame; this is called avidity.

'To insist that you know it all, that everything be done your way, snatching from others and appropriating for your own use; this is called avarice.

'To see your errors but refuse to change, to listen to remonstrance but go on behaving worse than before; this is called obstinacy.

'When men agree with you to commend them; when they disagree with you, to see no goodness in them, when it is there; this is called bigotry.'

'So,' spoke Counsellor Tang. 'When you, Teacher Chih-Po, can do away with the Eight Faults and avoid committing the

Four Evils, then and only then will you become capable of being taught. Before any man is qualified to evaluate another he must first be capable of being taught self-evaluation. Until that time you are dismissed for I have no need of services such as yours!'

⨎ Although never a day passes without our evaluating others, very few of us ever evaluate ourselves. Common sense tells us that we cannot evaluate another before we are able to evaluate ourselves, yet common practice proves otherwise. Judging the character of another is not a question of social status or seniority, though many people believe their 'position' enables them able to evaluate someone quickly. However, these same people have never evaluated themselves using the same criteria with which they evaluate others.

⨎ Those people who are responsible for regularly evaluating or appraising others will readily admit, if asked, that to be qualified to evaluate another, you first need to have evaluated your own thoughts and actions. Yet how many of them will want to admit that they have never actually done so themselves? Think for a moment about the people in the area you live in and the people you meet and work with: neighbours, colleagues, friends, customers, guests, new acquaintances and relatives. Consider the time you spend evaluating, appraising, analysing, assessing, considering or judging them. Now take a moment to reflect on the following: how much of each day do you spend in self-evaluation?

✱ Daily self-evaluation is the vital key to awakening your self-awareness. It is no use trying to imagine what awakened self-awareness is like before it is attained. Approach it the other way and see the result that non-awareness has on your life. Being unaware is like thinking that tomorrow will be different while you inwardly remain the same. Outer change demands inner change, and only through self-evaluation can we begin to see how to do things in a new way, a way that is beneficial. Nothing beneficial, however, can ever happen to us until we see something about ourselves that we were previously unaware of. Rather than ask, 'what can I do so that I can at last be happy?', we can ask 'what can I give up doing so that I can cease being unhappy?'

✱ Self-evaluation does not mean asking the opinions of others because there is always 'me as I am'; and 'me as I want others to think I am'. But regardless of the fact that our true-aware-self is the best friend and advisor we will ever have, we still tend to ask others – 'what do *you* think I should do?' rather than ask ourselves 'what must *I* do?'

✱ The questions we ask ourselves should be those that come so freely to us when silently evaluating others. For example, the next time you feel upset because you do not feel in control of a situation, ask yourself why you really need to have control. When someone annoys you because they always want the last word, ask yourself why it is that you are annoyed. Is it that you need to have the last word?

✗ Becoming aware involves standing outside of ourselves and observing everything that happens to us, both inside and out. In the same way that you have probably noticed how others fidget, drum their fingers or tap their feet, start to observe your own physical actions. Notice how you were unaware of them before.

✗ Many people unwittingly caught on camera are surprised to see how they fidget or gesture in a certain way, being previously unaware of it. When confronted with it, we are often surprised at the way we project ourselves to others. It is not some special gift for others to see us differently to the way we see ourselves; it is simply that we do not make the effort, or take the time, to be as aware of ourselves as we are of others.

Reacting and Responding

In the same way that we are aware of drinking hot or cold water, we can begin to make the same observations of our internal conditions by learning to distinguish between situations that cause us to become comfortably cool, or disturbingly hot. Observing how we react or respond to people and circumstances teaches us to address, rather than repress, the very cause of our reaction or response.

✗ Just the action of doing this leads us to greater self-awareness. The difference between reacting and responding is that in the former state you are not in control, whereas in the latter you are. It is important to register this difference because at any one moment in your life you are either in command of yourself or not. You either are, or you aren't. There is no neutral.

✤ Take the rejection or acceptance by another of what we do, for example. When another accepts us we respond positively. We feel in command because we feel needed, worthy and valued. If, however, we are rejected and we react negatively, it is because we feel unwanted, unworthy and unvalued. Unless we are aware that we are *re*acting to rejection we will merely repress whatever causes the feeling, thus inviting it to affect us whenever a similar situation threatens us.

✤ The very fact that we can be aware of our reaction, however, gives us the means to address it, thus destroying what causes it for ever. This follows the principle that to remove an illness you must first diagnose it. Awareness teaches us that we can actually learn more from rejection than from acceptance, in the same way that a missile stays on target because its gyro rejects a wrong direction.

Being Casually Alert

✤ The real art of effective contemplation is two-fold. It involves observing how the actions or emotions of others affect and influence you, and how your own actions and emotions affect others. Through consistent daily practice of observing how others react or respond, you can correct the actual causes which stem from your current thinking. Contemplation itself is the culmination of self-evaluation and detached observation.

✦ Imagine you have a dug a perfect hole. Now imagine you are simply passing a hole that someone else has dug, and as you do so you pause to inspect the hole. You are more dispassionate about the second hole because you have not dug it. The key is to try and imagine the first action with the emotion of the second. Any hole we dig ourselves into will always come from our own thinking, so being able to dispassionately contemplate why we have dug a hole and why we continue to put ourselves in it, enables us not only to get out of it but to fill it in for good.

✦ All negative thinking we harbour about ourselves will disappear unless it is held onto and given non-existent value. Dispassionate contemplation allows you to discard harmful thoughts from your mind in the same way that you discard out-of-date food. The increasing freedom you gain from self-defeating thoughts allows you to think more clearly.

✦ Clarity of thinking is fundamental to becoming aware of your inner world, and the more you understand your inner world the less your outer world can hurt you. Building greater awareness in your life requires you to be watchful of your daily affairs. This means learning to be *casually alert* in all things which, in turn, requires contemplation brought together with the second key.

Focused Attention

After twenty years in the service of a provincial overlord, a loyal soldier was rewarded. With enough money now to buy some acres of land, he was excited at being able to realise his dream of building his own home. For three whole months the soldier totally absorbed himself in preparing the land, clearing it of boulders and levelling the ground. He made sure that any wild bushes and neglected growth removed were replaced with trees and flowers. The work was long and hard but the soldier felt richly rewarded by thinking how pleasant his home would be.

While engrossed in what he was doing, a man came up to him and introduced himself as the land agent in the service of the local registrar.

'What so,' said the soldier taking the opportunity to rest, 'how can I be of service to you. All is well I trust?'

'I'm not sure,' said the man looking puzzled. 'Might I please enquire as to who has employed you on such obvious land improvement?'

'I am now in the service of my own,' replied the soldier proudly. 'I am the owner of this land I am preparing it for building.'

'There seems to have been some mistake,' said the land agent holding out some papers with some consternation. 'This is not your land, I'm afraid. Your land comprises the acres actually adjoining this.'

'Ah,' sighed the soldier. 'So, despite my endeavours I have not done a single thing to improve my own property.' And with that he immediately set to gathering his tools. The soldier took the

mistake in good spirits and after making sure that he was on his own land, he once more earnestly set about making his dream come true.

✯ If we are unaware that we are running down the wrong road then our attention to how fast we are running is irrelevant. Most times, though, we will not admit to ourselves that we are on the wrong road, so our thinking is never reversed and we continue to plough over old ground. Having attention in itself is a good discipline as it builds our ability to concentrate. But a difficult fact to accept is that one moment of awareness, in the right ground, is a thousand times better than one year of concentrated effort in the wrong ground. The 'wrong ground' denotes attraction which distracts us from self-awareness.

✯ The soldier in the story was so attracted to working towards his dream that he was distracted from ensuring that he was working the right land. When his error was pointed out, however, he immediately went to work without seeking redress for his error. And here is a vital truth, for when you are able to hear that all your work has been in vain without being angry, you are then on the path to self-awareness.

✯ Being able to focus your attention on what you should be doing, immediately you are aware of it, is preferable to the more common reaction of focusing attention on who was to blame for you not being aware.

✸ When people feel humiliation for having been cheated by others, for example, what really humiliates them is having their gullibility exposed. But a willingness to learn by being aware of why they feel the pain, will remove their gullibility. Yet most people do the opposite blaming external situations for their pain and seeking recompense to remove their humiliation. In doing so they merely trade the pain of the humiliation for the pain of resentment and anger.

✸ Blaming external conditions and other people for the way we feel is a major distraction from focusing on what we *really* want to do. Concentrating obsessively on making another pay for what we think they have done to us is the exact opposite of open concentration. It narrows our attention, drawing to us only those negative elements that will allow us to get our own back or make someone pay.

✸ When it comes to concentrating, our minds seem to travel like the movements of a snake - in order to travel straight ahead it moves from side to side. The span of our concentration on something that does not hold our attention is very short. This is usually because we are not aware of what it is that holds our attention. For example, a child's school report may declare that the child is unable to concentrate in class for two minutes without difficulty. This is the same child, however, that can concentrate endlessly on playing a game they have invented for themselves. It is simply that the latter holds their attention.

✸ Becoming aware as to when it is an effort to concentrate on something does not mean you should try harder to concentrate, it means acknowledging that what you are doing does not hold your attention. This is a clear opportunity to take the time to discover why.

✗ It may be that you are plain lazy. If that is the case then acknowledging it, rather than denying it, is the thing to do, as opportunities that are right for us begin to show up because our honest consciousness is ready for them, and as we are aware we notice them. A lazy person is often more innovative because they look to achieve things with the least possible effort.

✗ Alternatively, your attention may be lost simply because you have either lost interest, or were never interested in the first place. Often we refuse to be aware of this as it means acknowledging that we do what we do solely because of our commitments.

✗ Working at something because we *have* to, rather then because we *want* to, is definitely working the wrong ground. Putting good money into something that has failed in order to make it work is often viewed as something we have to do. With our attention on getting back what we may have lost, we concentrate on keeping whatever it is afloat.

✗ Being aware that it is not really what we want, however, can allow us to give it up by recognising our efforts are not serving any other purpose than maintaining our obstinacy or pride. Do not confuse these characteristics with persistence and determination as these qualities are vital for achievement.

The point is that unless we are fully aware of the emotions driving us, we may end up at the wrong destination.

✔ A state of heightened awareness allows us to ensure that we do not compromise what is best for us by accepting what is good. Having a 'good' job yet disliking it, is clearly not the 'best.' Concentrating on what is best for you has infinitely more focus than concentrating on what is just good. For example, concentrating your efforts on ensuring you can provide everything for your family may be at the expense of spending time together as a family; concentrating your efforts to ensure that you receive a promotion or contract may not be in your best health interests. What is *perceived* as best will be up to the individual's level of awareness.

✔ When something does hold your attention and absorbs you, then all ripple effects will be in your best interests because, in fully expressing yourself, you are 'walking your talk'. In this way your self-awareness, independent-will, creative-imagination and conscience are all acting in harmony.

Thinking Seriously Lightly

✔ As the best way of observing yourself is to be casually alert, then the best way to develop open concentration while focusing your attention is to take things *seriously lightly*. A state of heightened awareness does not recognise these as opposite concepts; they are the most natural and productive way of addressing everything.

✗ To think seriously lightly means to think from a position of understanding, rather than from the memories of past experiences. A person might think seriously about having lost a job, for example, but by resenting redundancy they rob themselves of thinking lightly, which could have produced peaceful understanding. Each time you consent to a loss, rather than resent it, expect a gain.

✗ The next time you have to concentrate on something important, first become aware of how you will feel about it. Take time to contemplate what you are about to do in order to establish if it is important to you as well as interesting and absorbing you. If your thoughts are positive then commence work in the full expectation that you will be gaining immense benefit from it.

✗ If the thoughts are negative, then contemplate why. It may be that you hunger for the credit rather than the personal satisfaction of seeing it through. If this is the case, by becoming aware of your need for recognition, you remove the distraction of it. You may become aware that this is not the way to proceed at all, in which case you have saved yourself further wasted effort. The numerous permutations of the truth will become clear, when you are self-aware.

✗ In actually applying your powers of concentration, go seriously lightly. In this way you will appreciate the whole of what you are doing and not close yourself off from the surrounding elements that are part and parcel of the task in hand. Too serious and you will not see the wood for the trees. Too light and you will see the wood without knowing the species of tree.

✣ For example, the proofreader who is concentrating purely on grammatical errors does not know the content of the book; the closeted judge concentrating on the psychology of the criminal mind has no time to understand about human nature; the religious scholar concentrating on performing rites and rituals overlooks spirituality; the businessman concentrating on satisfying his shareholders, never has time to meet his customers. Approaching everything with the seriously lightly attitude leads us to the application of the third key.

Witnessing Your Thoughts and Actions

A woman travelled to the great lake at Shura Province to seek the advice of a renowned sage. Granting her an audience, he enquired what she sought from him.

'I am here because my husband has talked of you with great respect,' began the woman. 'So, if I return with advice from yourself he may perhaps listen to it.'

'A man will only listen when he is ready to listen,' commented the sage, 'but you have travelled far, so tell me the problem you have.'

'My husband is a high court judge. But he remains so every moment, even in bed. I have not known a lover, friend or husband. He is always so proud of how alert and aware he is of everything and everyone, yet, for twenty-four hours a day he is aware of nothing, except being a high court judge. It is said

that you have the power to allow people to see themselves as others do. Please can you help me?'

'Often the height of the pedestal prevents removal from it,' began the sage, 'whatever a person does; be they a scholar, merchant or emperor. But I will help you. Return and tell him that you have received word, albeit from my own lips, that I have heard of his respect for me and will therefore pay my own to him soon.'

Hearing the news that such a renowned sage would be visiting his house, the high court judge placed a sentry to give him early warning of his arrival. 'It is because he has heard of my alert mind that he is visiting,' he told his colleagues while inviting them to come also.

The town merchants and scholars looked forward to the day. The clerks to the judge felt more important than before as they answered the townspeople's questions: 'Of course such a sage will not visit just anyone, you know. The reputation of our master's wisdom goes far and wide, for there are none that challenge it.'

When the sentry reported that a stranger asking where the high court judge lived had entered the town, word quickly spread and within the hour the House of Justice was bursting at the seams.

But the stranger was not the sage. He was a simpleton who, when questioned, replied that he had been sent ahead by the sage to test the judge's renowned wisdom. If the judge answered four questions from the simpleton incorrectly then the sage would come. If, however, the judge was to answer any of the questions correctly, then the judge would lose the test and the sage would not come.

'*Some test,*' thought the judge. '*Answering incorrectly is far easier than answering correctly. How can I lose with this confused simpleton?*' Then, speaking out loud for the benefit of all, he said, '*Begin your test, ask your questions all of which I will answer incorrectly for you. When I pass you must bring your master and should I lose, well if I were to, I would even give you ten gold coins from my own purse.*'

So the simpleton began, and asked, '*Where do you come from?*'

The Judge said, '*From Chao Province,*' which was incorrect as he had always lived in Shura Province. '*There,*' he said, winking at his clerks, '*I have passed the first test.*'

'*How long have you been here?*' asked the simpleton for his second question.

'*Two weeks only,*' replied the Judge, who had lived there all his life, among growing laughter as people began to join in on the joke.

The third time the simpleton asked: '*Our courts are fair and just in this province. Do you agree?*'

'*Not at all,*' answered the Judge. '*Our Courts are the worst in all China,*' again passing the test.

'*It seems that you can't lose,*' said the simpleton, '*you are as aware as they say you are. How many questions have I asked so far?*'

The judge said, '*you have asked me three questions; you have one more. If I do not answer it correctly I pass your master's tests.*'

'*Look!*' cried out the simpleton, jumping up and down with excitement. '*The judge has failed the test. He has answered this question correctly! You see when great judges are not alert they lose. Had he been more aware he would have passed the test.'*

Having his pride smashed in front of his peer group had an enormous impact on the judge. In the silence that engulfed the entire room, he entered momentarily a trance-like state where he became a witness to the whole event. He did not feel a victim; he was simply witnessing the absurdity of what had been a false-self that relied on a pedestal, title, respect and importance. Returning to his quarters later, the high court judge felt lighter as if a huge burden had been lifted from him. He became aware of the warm welcome from his wife as he opened the door.

⨎ This story illustrates one of the most important secrets of living with fulfilment – to be able to witness ourselves, rather than judge. Everybody is capable of reaping the infinite benefits available, yet most don't even get close to it; we are too busy judging others. Although each of us carries the key to the door of fulfilment, very few ever turn the lock.

⨎ Taking the time to meditate is often all that is required. The perception of sitting cross-legged and half-naked under a tree humming to yourself is not meditation. Millions of people, though, miss out on meditation because of its false connotation. They think it is gloomy and serious, or religious and monastic, or downright weird and bizarre. Yet meditation affords the opportunity to embark on the greatest adventure the human mind can take. In truth, total awareness is a form of meditation.

To meditate means to become a witness. That's the whole secret of meditation – you become the watcher of whatever you are doing. Action is not the purpose, but the quality that you bring to your action. Walking, sitting, running, jogging and swimming are all forms of meditation if you remain alert. Meditation is a quality that can be brought to *anything*; it is not a specific act.

The common belief, however, is that it must be a specific act; you must sit facing east, repeat certain mantras, burn some incense in a particular way at a particular time. Meditation has nothing to do with anything that seeks to automate it because it is not about automation, it is about alertness. So long as you can keep alert, any activity can be a meditation.

The key to meditating does involve a *knack*. A knack is not a science or an art; it cannot be taught. But effort is required to acquire the knack. Learning to swim or ride a bike takes initial effort before it becomes natural. When you have the knack, however, you never forget, despite any infrequency of use. Regular swimming or cycling will improve ability but once you have 'clicked' with how to maintain buoyancy or balance respectively, what was once a locked door is always open to you.

Although meditation is not in itself a technique, there are numerous techniques to achieve the heightened awareness that it brings. You can learn by yourself, but the journey can be tedious and boring. Techniques used in thousands of years of experiments can certainly save you unnecessary groping about and propel your growth immensely. If after trying one for a few days, nothing 'clicks,' then try another. You will know when one is right for you as you will feel right about using it.

✝ In the beginning meditating will seem like an effort. When you succeed, the effort disappears and the whole thing becomes spontaneous, like breathing. Effort is always required in the beginning because the mind will not start anything without it. A moment will come when through your effort you relax and effortlessly become a witness. In this meditative state, you are beyond the thinker in you, beyond what you are doing, you are just aware.

✝ Looking at the whole of something is an example of awareness. Whenever we look at an object or person, although unconsciously, we look at the parts. Taking a bowl of fruit, for example. We move our eyes to look at the sides, then to what it contains, then to the substance. But by refusing to allow our eyes to divide what they see into parts we force them to see something as a whole. Try it. First look at any object, a wall picture perhaps. Notice how you look from one part to another. Then suddenly look at it as a whole; do not divide it. Do not allow your eyes to move. Do not think; forget the substance, material or what the frame is made of, just look at the form.

¥ Continue looking at the form as a whole, and in a few moments you become aware of yourself because your eyes are not allowed to move outwards. The form has been taken as a whole, so you cannot move to the parts. As the eyes demand movement, so your vision will move towards you and suddenly you will become aware of watching yourself watch the object. This will give you an indication of what being a witness rather than a judge involves.

Meditating

¥ It is important when you are new to meditation to allow yourself enough time and to find a peaceful place. The half-hour you take out of the occasional twenty-four hour day will prove to be more valuable to you than the rest, although you may not believe it now. Certainly tranquillity is important so you may prefer to rise earlier than usual in order to enjoy some quiet time alone. When a person has really learned to meditate, however, they can meditate anywhere and anytime with no concern of distraction.

¥ There are two distinct meditations that have proved to be successful. One form that has led more people to a state of heightened awareness than any other is *Vipassana*. As there is nothing to add or subtract anything from it, you can only improve it. As nothing during the meditation is considered a distraction, it is ideal for many beginners. There are two favoured methods. The first involves awareness of your body, your mind and your mood. The second involves awareness of your breathing. Both can be performed while either sitting or walking.

✗ Adopt a comfortable and alert position to sit for twenty minutes. Back and head should be straight, eyes closed, and breathing normal. This means breathing down to the stomach and not through raising the chest. If you are uncertain, practise lying on the floor with your hand just above your navel. When it rises up and down you are breathing correctly. Your focus of attention should be on watching the rise and fall of your stomach caused by the in and out of your breathing.

✗ If you are distracted by anything including thoughts, feelings, judgements, body sensations and impressions from the outside world, pay attention to whatever is happening until it is possible to make breathing your focus again. It is the process of watching that is important, not what you are watching so do not identify with whatever your thoughts are. Problems and questions should pass like ships on the horizon. It is only when you identify with a ship that you feel distressed. If you say, 'that is my ship', you will worry as soon as it passes from sight. When negative ideas arise just watch them and let them go.

✗ The alternative method involves an ordinary walk, focusing on your feet touching the ground. You can walk in a circle or a line of ten to fifteen steps going back and forth, inside or out of doors. Your eyes should be focused on the ground a few steps ahead. While walking, your focus of attention should go to the contact of each foot as it touches the ground. If you are diverted, stop paying attention to the feet, notice what else took your attention and then return to the feet. Walk for twenty minutes.

🌱 *Zazen* Meditation is the other distinct form. It involves just sitting. Doing absolutely nothing is hard, but once you have the knack many things will begin to happen. At first, and possibly for several weeks, incessant thoughts of the pointlessness of what you are doing, will enter your mind. 'How can you waste so much time, when you could be earning money?' your mind will demand. 'You could at least do something, even if it is just watching TV. Entertain yourself, this is absurd.'

🌱 Your mind will do all that it can to stop you from just sitting. It will make you sleepy, or want to move, or come up with a million arguments and reasons for not staying put. But if you can just persevere, the mind eventually stops its haranguing. Sit anywhere – so long as you are not distracted – in front of a plain wall is ideal. Adopt a good posture, ensuring you can remain comfortably still for twenty minutes. This is important because if the body does not move, the mind calms. Your eyes should be half open, allowing your gaze to rest softly on the wall, and your breathing should be relaxed. Place your attention at a spot behind the centre of your forehead, where the pineal gland is located, but do not concentrate. Remain relaxed while becoming receptive and alert from moment to moment.

Enlightenment

✣ Meditation may seem difficult at first but the rewards are worth the effort. The key is patience. The very nature of meditation is non-goal orientated, so more than anything else the meditator has to work on the process without attachment to the result. At times impatience will come, as impatience always comes with the thirst for achievement. But the meditator must learn to throw away patience while keeping his or her thirst. With thirst there is yearning but no struggle; with impatience there is struggle but no yearning. Truth cannot be raided; it is attained through surrender, not through struggle.

✣ Meditation masters the unruly mind very effectively. Command of your mind, and being aware of your thinking, will determine your success in everything you undertake. How can the aeons of heritage, tradition, conditioning and prejudice that have allowed the mind to believe it is the master of you rather than your servant, be overcome just by doing nothing and watching? It can, because like the night-watchmen keeping thieves at bay with his light, destructive thoughts are vanquished when they are seen for what they are. A negative thought is like a thief, it does not like to be in the spotlight. As the watcher grows stronger and more aware he becomes at one with the strengthening light his awareness brings. That is the meaning of enlightenment. At one with the Light. At one with the Truth. Where we can use our judgement instead of being judgemental.

Relaxed Intensity

✢ Observing yourself through self-evaluation, focusing your attention through open concentration and witnessing your thoughts and actions through meditation are the valuable keys to creating a state of *relaxed intensity*. Here again, higher consciousness does not recognise opposites, it sees them as complementary energies. Concentration itself is the key to all aspects of life. The more you concentrate on what you do, the more you begin to live in the present. Whenever you lack concentration you are easily distracted from living in the present, and distractions are the enemy of awareness.

✢ When you increase your levels of concentration you begin to see yourself in a different light. You re-channel your nervous energy, using it to work with you, not against you. But the true power of concentration is the ability to become a witness to your own being. To achieve this means that you must learn to relax while at the same time focusing your concentration. Meditation, or even just taking the time to reflect, is calmness, relaxing; while concentration is intensity, doing. One is not the other but together they create a state of relaxed-intensity.

✢ Action through non-action and doing without doing is ancient wisdom. Each complements the other, making the whole stronger. Remember that concentration is focusing the mind on form; contemplation is focusing the mind on an idea; and meditation is raising the consciousness. Spending time on each regularly will allow you to attain a level of awareness that will prove enlightening in all aspects of perception, situations, opportunities and witnessing.

✶ As you shine the light of attention back in on yourself, rather than on external devices and skills which are only visible reflections of yourself, your whole sense of perspective will be clearer. You will know the direction to take in all matters, opportunities will come to you without effort, and you will know what to do with them.

Holding the Carp

Cultivating Your Superconscious

'To be out of Trader's City and fishing feels good,' exclaimed Su-Lei, 'it was a fine idea of yours. Let us hope the carp are as big here as you say.'

'Of course they are,' said Wing, 'for carp are like ideas. They expand in relation to their limitations. They grow twice as big in a large lake such as this one, as they do when they are contained.'

'But we have some enormous carp that swim in a tank at our House of Trade,' protested Su-Lei.

'Ah, but they are imported from the lakes,' answered his friend, 'like imported ideas to have around us. Their spawn stay small because of their contained environment, like so many conditioned ideas.'

Su-Lei cast his line across the lake as he considered his friend's words. 'Though we are good at getting on with things, it is true we lack some bright ideas. Sometimes we get one but...look! I have hooked a big one.' Su-Lei excitedly pulled in his line, which was taut as the large fish strained to free itself. Holding it still in his hands a few minutes later to remove his hook, the captive suddenly jumped, slipping out of his hands and back in the water before he could stop it. 'It's gone, I had it and lost it and it was a good one too,' said Su-Lei with frustration.

'Were you still talking about your ideas, or your fish,' offered a bemused Wing.

'Ah, and just so,' replied Su-Lei. 'Ideas can be like a slippery fish. It seems that unless one holds tight, what one has will get away, ready to be caught by another with a firmer hand. Why, only the other day I saw something selling at the market which will bring much fortune to the trader. Yet, at the same time I recognised it as the culmination of an idea that had come to me months before. If only the timing had been better for me and I had not been so busy, it could have been my product.'

'But it did come at the right time,' said Wing, 'as the answer to what we want does every time. Your inner guide, Su-Lei, is there to aid you with everything, including your decision making. Problems only come when we fight against our inner sage, second guess it, or never hold on to what it says because we are too busy.'

'That's all very well,' argued Su-Lei, 'but being in business successfully means being busy — a busy man catches more fish, as they say. But how do you recognise this "sage" and its "answer" from all the voices that occupy the mind?'

'By daring to ask it the right questions of course!' answered Wing.

⅄ From ancient times there has been talk of the human mind being part of a more powerful mind, a Universal Mind.

Access to this mind is understood to be through our superconscious, the very medium for our soul's awareness of everything. Our enthusiasm and excitement, our intuition and insight, our creativity and imagination, and our motivation and inspiration are influenced by this genius each of us has the power to draw from.

✤ Genius is considered rare, simply because Man is not consciously aware that he has the capacity for it. Yet everyone without exception has had an idea come to them and done nothing about it, only to see its physical reality months, or years, later. That experience alone signifies that each of us has a connection to a wider world than just our conscious mind. There is an inexhaustible wealth of potential within us, just waiting to be tapped into.

✤ We all have voices in our minds. Often they are the internalised voices of our parents, teachers, and both significant and insignificant others who have influenced us during our formative years. Some of our inner voices are helpful and supportive, others are demanding and critical, often unhelpfully so. Listening to these voices can severely contain us within fixed limits, not allowing us to expand to our full potential.

✤ It is, therefore, important to distinguish between the critic within, which must be silenced, and the guide within, which must be cultivated. This guide can be likened to a sempiternal sage who, though he has lived forever, keeps up to date on current events in the lives of people. Being able to recognise and interpret our sage is one of the most important factors for expanding our boundaries and taking charge of our lives.

⊁ It is through the superconscious that our intuitive faculty comes, a faculty that can be deliberately cultivated and consciously trained. Intuition is a capacity each of us is born with, like the capacity for breathing and eating. For most of our lives we are not consciously aware of them. When we do take care to breathe properly, our physiology improves dramatically, indeed lymphatic functions, essential to our health, improve over one thousand percent. When we take care to eat properly, our mental and emotional well-being improves significantly.

⊁ Reclaiming conscious control over your innate powers increases them. As you read the pages of this book, for example, you are using a series of complex mental functions without being consciously aware that you are doing so. One of these functions, your memory, instantaneously compares each word you read with countless words stored in your memory bank. Associations and images are continuously served up, with the word's meaning, into your conscious mind. Similarly, intuition continuously serves up data to your conscious mind, even though you're completely unaware of the process. The key is to learn how to become conscious of this.

⊁ We were given intuition for a reason. Like our other senses it is first and foremost a survival tool. Our ancestors' daily survival depended on how tuned in they were to their surroundings; the most intuitive survived. Intuitions arise as they are needed and are meant to guide us. As a survival skill, intuition is especially adept at addressing the future. For most of us the process of gathering information not immediately available, takes place unconsciously, and with a lot of interference from our rationalising logic and our emotional impulsiveness. The important fact is that in being consciously intuitive, our ability to make accurate decisions is significantly improved.

🗲 It is a misconception that intuition is a power we acquire, as it is already an integral part of our psyche. A further myth is that women are more intuitive than men. This misconception is based on the belief that the former come up with intuitive solutions more consistently. In the same way that men have been taught to show their strengths while women have been taught to hide theirs, men may refer to hunches and gut feelings, rather than admit to intuitive insights until recently associated with feminine realms

🗲 The bizarre fact is, the less you know about a subject or topic, the more intuition comes into play. A partner, regardless of sex, can know the right course of action when their advice is asked for, because they are removed from it. In being so they are able to heed their intuition as part of their decision making, rather than be persuaded to ignore it, because of the weight of solid evidence.

🗲 The skill, however, is to combine our intuitive powers with our powers of reason and feeling to improve decision making. Decision-making should involve intellect, emotion *and* intuition: does it add up, does it feel right and does it *sound* right? Mathematical analysis, for example, should only get us to the point where our intuition takes over. Yet although everyone is intuitive, only a few learn how to access and interpret it.

✴ We live in an age where the limitations of traditional logic and rational guidance have become clearer to see. Increasingly, proactive individuals and businesses are no longer dismissing our natural modes of guidance as something intangible and unreliable. What was formerly considered as solely a feminine attribute is being rediscovered as a rigorous method fundamental to future survival as well as meaningful and valued growth.

✴ An intuitive is simply someone who consciously uses intuition in his or her personal and professional life. We all use our intuition unconsciously, which is why the promptings that come from our sagely guide are so faintly heard at first. Even though they are clearly audible on their own plane, we tend to disregard them as trivial. This is the tragedy of Man. The voices that so often misguide him into pain and self-limitation are both loud and clamorous. The whisper that guides him to material and spiritual harmony is timid and soft. Cultivating our superconscious allows us to develop our particular intuitive strengths from an unlimited source outside our general experience. Such deliberate cultivation requires the conscious practise of three important keys.

Confidently Trusting

'Forgive me my General,' said Ho-Yen, 'but you look greatly troubled these days. How so? Is this battle not just another skirmish for you?'

'I fear that the state of Kou-Wu will soon be no more, for our rivals have great strength,' answered the General.

'Allow me to suggest my lord that you enquire of the oracle of Zig-Zag Mountain,' offered Ho-Yen. 'It is said that his foresight is never wrong. With an answer in hand, you will know how to fight.'

'Surely that sagely legend holds no truth, although I would seek any advice at this time,' sighed the General, 'for I am uncertain as to what tactics to follow for the best.'

Having travelled to Zig-Zag Mountain Ho-Yen reminded the General, just before he was about to enter the mystic cave alone, that he could only ask one question of the oracle.

'Indeed, I have only one question,' replied the General, 'and it is the one I have been asking myself for days now as ten thousand troops gather. Will this great battle be won?'

Many months later a very bedraggled Ho-Yen was found on Zig-Zag Mountain by the oracle's disciple, employed in gathering herbs.

'What has happened for you to lie so forlorn on the track leading to my master's cave?' he asked.

'Your master was wrong,' said Ho-Yen bitterly, 'and I came to tell him so. He answered yes to our great general, yet the battle was lost! Kou-Wu is no more, it belongs to the province of Yuen.'

'Forgive me honourable sir, but in truth my master answered correctly,' said the disciple. *'A great battle was won, even though the victor was your general's rival.'*

'But it was I who suggested bringing him to this infernal place,' said Ho-Yen. *'He came here trusting he would receive an answer to his benefit, not his ill.'*

'Yet to come here is to not trust yourself, for my master speaks only what other men already know but lack the confidence to accept,' said the disciple. *'Had your general asked the right questions of himself he would have received the answer on the right course of action. Had he trusted himself he would have asked more specifically. As my master says: Be careful what you ask for in life.'*

'I believe at the end he knew the truth,' said Ho-Yen resignedly. *'As he lay wounded he told me: "Good friend, in truth no agency can be trusted better than your own source, no matter how great it is. I refused to trust my own, so refrained from asking it, in case it told me something I did not want to hear. What use are ten thousand troops when a man leading them cannot follow himself?".'*

✱ It is a paradoxical truth that the best leaders are the best followers, and only when we confidently trust our own inner guidance do we become able to lead ourselves. Yet it is difficult to find the right answer after years of schooling have conditioned us to fear questions. Many people fear filling out intrusive forms, part and parcel of our information demanding society, because of the pressure of putting down what has to be the right answer.

✗ As the world is becoming increasingly specialised, it is more difficult to remain an informed participant. We hand over decisions to experts and specialists who know better. In doing so it becomes unnecessary for us to rely on our own infallible guidance power, and subsequently we trust it less and less. Many people become unable to make decisions concerning their lives without the opinion of others, whom they in turn blame when things go wrong. It is largely the questions we ask ourselves that makes the life of one person different from another. Thus, the important thing in life is knowing what questions we should be asking.

✗ A question effectively phrased can already be half answered. Ambiguous questions that be interpreted in more than one way. Will I be happy? Should I go into business? Will I get married? Should I move jobs? Will I have enough money? These kinds of questions that all of us ask of some 'oracle' at one time or another during our lives, are not specific. But it is not just a matter of good grammatical English and syntax. Questions need to have received investment from feeling, emotion and logic. The famous Delphic Oracle in the very birthplace of logic and rational philosophy, ancient Greece, illustrates that rational thought and intuitive thinking can support each other.

✗ The key is to use the intuitive part of the mind and the reasoning part as a team, rather than one against the other. Both are necessary as yin is to yang, female to male, emotion to logic. Intuition tells us what to do, while reason tells us how to go about doing it, helping us to find, clarify, determine and research. It is important to understand that the two are to work together, whilst recognising and accepting each other's peculiar characteristics and different methods of approach. One moves in a non-linear fashion, the other in a rigid sequence pattern.

✼ Hence, all projects formed should be examined under this duplex light, which is infinitely better than our habit of always asking others what they think. In performing the latter we consistently refuse to build the self-confidence we need to even take our own advice, let alone heed it.

✼ The truth is that it is an unnatural condition not to know which way to turn when we are faced with different courses of action to pursue. If the fault of this lies within us, then the correction must lie within us also. Put simply, it is a great pity that we do not have second thoughts first. Not trusting our own intuition comes from not believing in ourselves, or believing that we do not really deserve what we would like to happen. In asking 'should I go into business, or should I take the new job,' for example, we are immediately saying that we have not thought out what we really want.

✼ It is important to understand why we want to make a move and what we think it will do for us. This raises personal questions such as: does the kind of security and compensation I can expect fit in with my primary goals – those things that are important to me? Should I take this job if I want to spend more time with my family? Will this move provide me with the experience I am seeking?

✴ Intuition is activated in response to questions and is goal-directed. But as it responds by presenting us with impressions and images, we must be consciously aware of our questions in order to understand the signs it gives us. Otherwise, and this is what usually happens, we send out conflicting signals. For example: 'I want to earn more, but I don't want more responsibility'; 'I want a rise, yet I want more time with my family'; 'I want a relationship, yet I like my independence,' are demands that we are not often conscious of expressing.

✴ In Western thinking, answers follow questions. With intuition, questions follow answers. A question will raise impressions which in turn suggest more questions. But it will do so in a non-linear fashion, not in the more rigid sequence associated with reason. So it is important to be absolutely clear about what we are consciously asking and why. In this way, we can understand and interpret the impressions we receive and be prepared to address the new questions that subsequently arise. In leaving one job or relationship for another, an intuitive answer may pose the question that there is something we must fundamentally change about the way we are going through life.

✴ As there is no stronger soul to direct us than our own, it is important to build the self-confidence to trust ourselves. This can only be done through developing clarity of purpose and understanding the motives behind the goals we want to achieve. In essence this means working towards being consistently true to ourselves. The degree to which we are, is in direct proportion to how tuned in we are with the Universal Mind and its infinite storehouse of knowledge.

✱ When we are busy being somebody for everybody, we can neither be ourselves nor trust ourselves. As we are unable to trust what our inner guide unerringly advises, we allow our preconceived opinions, formed of intellectual pride, prejudices and beliefs, to build a barrier. With this barrier standing in the way of true wisdom we look upon others as masters and sources, instead of the teachers and agencies they really are. Developing a confident trust in ourselves through clarity of question and a willingness to interpret our intuition, however absurd it may initially seem, is academic, of course, unless there is adherence to the second key.

Sincerely Listening

'If only you had contacted me earlier,' said Counsellor Tang. 'You would have been welcome to have had the position. Indeed, it would have made my job considerably easier. But please understand that I cannot change what I have now done. The seal has been set and, of course, it would be unfair for the new licensee.'

Merchant Fou-Ha was livid with himself. How could he have been so stupid not to have followed up his strong impression of last month? That license was just what he wanted, but how could it be that Counsellor Tang was the authority to grant it? Why, it wasn't even his province, which is why he had ignored the inclination to go to him. He had not listened to it, reasoning that if he asked Counsellor Tang, then the whole court would know and he would certainly lose all opportunity of obtaining such a licence.

'Perhaps the new licensee may consider negotiating with you.' suggested the Counsellor. 'I don't believe he has the experience you have so indeed may welcome the alliance.'

Merchant Fou-Ha's anger started to turn towards what he considered was utterly unfair. He began to feel outrage, reasoning that the two had obviously cheated him out of what should have been his. In the instant before letting rip a verbal rendition of what he thought of this bureaucrat's heritage, he sensed another impression. Almost like a voice, it urged him to keep quiet and not say something that he would later regret. But his anger overruled the voice and the cutting words were already out, quickly flying to their mark. With chilling accuracy they hit it. Almost immediately they were regretted.

'Ho Sir!' exclaimed the Counsellor in surprise. 'Such dragon's teeth as those should be removed. To dare to question my authority is one thing, to slur the name of my ancestors is one more. The sum of both will cost you dear!'

Later Fou-Ha rationalised that his words, although said in the heat of the moment, had been well deserved. Following his outburst he had ignored his feeling to ask for forgiveness, reasoning that it would only show further weakness. His silence had compounded the situation and now he faced a heavy fine.

'It could have been worse you know,' commented his friend, Trader Yen. 'He is clearly a fair counsellor to show such leniency in the loss of so much face. Perhaps he thinks you have lost more.'

'What does it matter what he thinks,' said Merchant Fou-Ha,

'I am worse off than ever thanks to him. First I don't get the licence for not talking to him, then I get a fine for talking to him. Some counsellor!'

'With respect,' replied his friend, 'I feel that I am unable to agree with you. Your whole problem has nothing to do with you talking, or not talking. It has to do with you hearing, but not sincerely listening.'

Ϡ Every one of us experience the feeling or urge to contact someone. It may be someone in authority, for example, and we choose not to act preferring to let 'sleeping dogs lie.' Often, the very next day, or at least soon after, we receive a letter or phone call from that very same person. We kick ourselves for not having contacted them first, annoyed at being pre-empted, giving away the advantage. Sometimes we do take the initiative, but delay in contacting someone only to learn that the person had been thinking of us earlier. People in tune with each other will often make contact at about the same time about the same thing. The fact is that all of us hear what to do, but only a few listen.

Ϡ Preferring to go with what we think we ought to or should do, we delay and thus obscure our feeling. We then invite other mistaken, conflicting beliefs to provide reasons for not following our intuition. So, although everybody hears their intuition, most people spend their time reasoning out why they can't do something, instead of intuitively finding out how they can. There is both good sense and reason for the Eastern belief that the less you do, the more you achieve, until you reach the point where in doing nothing, you accomplish everything.

❦ What underlies this is the belief that when you are in tune with the Universal Mind, everything flows in the best way. If you apply this wisdom to the business world, its truth will be revealed. Seasoned successful executives, for example, do less than they did when they were climbing the ladder of success, yet achieve considerably more. As they follow their 'hunches' so they have more time available to think, without the company of others. Being highly productive rarely involves high activity, yet often activity is mistaken for productivity.

❦ The majority of people do not take the time to retreat from the company of others in order to get ideas and inspiration. They are too busy doing what they do to become what they can. When people prefer to confer with everybody and everything else but themselves, they fail to tap into their innate superconscious for inspiration. Many go to great lengths not to be alone, to be always surrounded by others. Yet only by developing our aloneness can we learn to tune into our inspirational power. Despite the proven fact that one flash of insight can clear up a thousand difficulties, people continue to be active in addressing each difficulty one by one.

❦ Having time alone is not about being lonely. It is a beneficial solitude and provides by far the best way to learn how to activate your voice of inner guidance. It is possible, with practice, to hear this voice to the point that you recognise it regardless of surrounding noise. But to begin, there must be solitude. Ask yourself how often you take the time to be completely alone without any artificial influences whatsoever, and just listen to your own thoughts, without going to sleep.

¥ Tens of thousands of travelling business people have the perfect opportunity to do this. Yet on the plane they eat, talk, watch a video or sleep; on a train they read, talk, phone or dine; immediately on entering a hotel room they turn on the television, computer, pick up the phone or return to the company of others as soon as possible.

¥ Recognising that the majority of the best ideas come while 'out of the office', has led many businesses to attend executive 'retreats'. These are great opportunities to talk, share ideas, discuss strategy, plan future objectives, develop shared values, improve processes and systems, plan to increase productivity, reduce in-house politics, bond team members, motivate, inspire and improve communication. But do they? They are highly effective because they put people in a different environment, but they are seldom retreats. Most are simply boardrooms out of the office, where the intention is that participants can remain undisturbed, though in reality this is not the case. Even the rooms at the venue are set up to look the same as the office, because that is what is expected.

¥ Moreover, despite the prior understanding that attention should be on the process of the retreat, most people are unable to comply. The common excuse for this is, 'I'm sorry, but I must stay in contact with the office as they might need me for something important.' So each coffee-break is used as an opportunity to phone the office. With faxed and internet messages, countless calls to take and make, and lots of time in the bar to discuss problems back at the office, there is seldom the opportunity to retreat.

✔ In our information-driven world, where technology allows us to perform a hundred tasks in the time it used to take to perform one, we still do not have the time to develop those invaluable inspirations that will propel a business way beyond what was previously imagined possible.

✔ This state of affairs encourages people to live at a breakneck pace, with the days and nights crowded with things to be done or things to distract us from doing. Aloneness, not loneliness, is often very difficult to procure, and many would feel unhappy if they had it. Some of us cannot bear silence or being alone for more than a few minutes. Indeed, some organisations unable to play music, play a background 'white' noise in order that there should be no embarrassing silence during meetings.

✔ Outside the office environment, a new syndrome has arisen for the 'teleworker'. A growing number of people working from home develop 'loneliness' symptoms though lack of interaction with others. But loneliness, regardless of environment, is ultimately a state of mind. Having to redevelop a relationship with one's self through the opportunity to be alone is to be embraced, not feared.

🗡 Amazingly enough, the deep silence of a quiet place is something many of us have never known. Most will argue that they haven't the time because their responsibilities fill every waking hour. Yet a greater responsibility is to reorganise our lives so that we are able to retreat to a quiet place, and once more learn how to get in touch with our self, simply through listening.

🗡 Indeed, by calling a halt, being still and listening, our loads are lightened. We see how best to complete our work without struggle, less effort and with greater enjoyment. The flashes of inspiration that bring us what we want are just that. They are more responsible for propelling the world toward solutions than the constant hustle and bustle involved in trying to find answers through external means.

🗡 Arguably, most of the above is plain common sense. But when it comes to developing our innate powers, what is common sense is not common practice. Despite recognising the fact that deep down each of us has an intuitive power that will unerringly guide us, we deliberately choose not to develop it. Instead, we promise ourselves the time to develop it in the future, for we are too busy to think about it today.

🗡 We have to resolve to build the habit of sincerely listening to ourselves everyday. This is important, as all intuitive guidance is like manna in the desert and needs to be acted on as it occurs. The less you embark on your daily retreat, the more you will come to loathe it. If you are unable to develop the time to go mentally fishing for a set period each day, then it is doubtful that you will catch any worthwhile ideas. Conversely, the more you embark on your daily retreat, the more you will come to like it. In developing the habit you will discover that you become more accustomed to listening, and therefore receptive, to your intuitive voice.

✝ This is not because your intuition is talking to you more; it is because you are becoming more accustomed to recognising how it speaks to you. It may come in the form of signals, impressions, symbols, objects, reading a book, talking to another, idly noticing something or a strong urge. The secret is to stop, on the instant, whatever you are doing, or saying at that moment and reorient all your attention to the message. The incomplete act, the broken sentence, should be left, for this is an exercise in evaluating something sincerely.

✝ That is the real secret for developing your connection to the superconscious - learning how to shift your attention when you feel, notice, or become aware of an intuitive message. You shift your attention by listening with absolute sincerity, the same sincerity you would bring to your marriage vows. For, in truth, they have the same value. The guidance coming through to you is that spiritual part that only wants the very best for you, as one who loves another would want. And, as in the building of all relationships, that involves the third key, risk.

Faithfully Risking

A traveller who had recently entered a foreign province was accosted suddenly by another traveller who told him in a frightened voice, 'We have wasted our time in this direction, for behind those dark clouds is a vast mountain which will block our way.'

The first traveller felt strangely calm, a calmness that he had not fully experienced before. A while ago he would have reacted with great concern, but this time he felt no artificial sense of impending doom. Surprised at the report, though, he thanked the frightened traveller and continued on his journey to see whether it was true or not.

He came upon no mountain, but he did meet another stranger who reported gloomily, 'It is hopeless to continue your journey. Just beyond that meadow is a precipitous canyon that even the nimblest of goats are unable to cross.'

Once more experiencing a sense of inner calm, the traveller decided to see for himself and went on his way leaving the stranger disapprovingly shaking his head. There was no canyon at all on the path he took, but he did run into a third stranger in a military uniform, who sternly commanded, 'Stop! You are forbidden to go any further in this direction. This path leads straight into the camp of an army that will punish your attempts to continue.'

Not frightened by the threat the traveller walked passed the fuming stranger. He met with no camp and there were no soldiers to block his path. Travelling on his way he encountered a fourth traveller. But this person seemed no stranger, indeed the man felt as if he was entering the presence of a long-lost friend. As he approached, the other traveller extended his arms in welcome, saying, 'Because you decided to take no-one's word for anything, but to test everything on yourself, my wait has been brief.'

'But, tell me,' asked the traveller, 'who are you, although I feel sure I know you. Have we met before?'

'Of course,' came the answer, 'I am your faithful guide for life. What you have risked confirmed your faith in me so I am able to become fully present. Come, let us continue, there is no insurmountable obstacle ahead and so much to share with you.'

✔ We will recognise the voice of wisdom when having to make a decision, by the fact that it emanates from deep inner calm. Impulse, on the other hand, is frequently born of undue excitement. The intuitive traveller need not fear nor hesitate when meeting strange things which try to block his or her journey. The key is to simply be aware that they are there, both inside and outside, and walk right past them.

✔ Learning to faithfully risk the guidance of our intuition requires us to be like Bunyan's Pilgrim who met and left behind impeding temptations. Understanding that there is no-one who has any real power over you other than yourself, allows you to pass beyond every fearful obstacle and travel forwards.

✝ Confidence in one's self is built through risk. We must be ready to risk mistakes because we may not always have the right intuition. If we disbelieve the intuition, however, then we will not have it at all. Nothing of any meaningful consequence can be attained without risk. Indeed, the greater risk can often be in not taking a risk, for whatever is necessary for us to do, is also *possible* for us to do. Risk builds faith and in turn faith allows us to risk. When we become accustomed to faithfully-risking that which the powerful superconscious affords, we overcome ourselves. In overcoming ourselves, we overcome the world.

✝ There is no single pattern that an intuitively guided life must follow. Sometimes we will see, in a flash of insight, both our course and destination. But at other times we will only see the next step ahead and will have to keep an open mind, both as to the second step, and as to the final destination. It is at these times that one must believe in one's self enough to risk the second step in the faith that, although the answer may not always come when we need it, it will always come when the occasion calls for it.

✝ Whenever we reason or feel that we are taking a risk by following what we intuitively think, we should do so anyway. Even if we are later proved mistaken, it is the only way to practise and develop the level of confidence and faith in ourselves essential for our intuitive capabilities to fully present themselves in the long-term.

The Right Hook for Certainty

✷ There are opposites in all things, and in everything there exists the spirit of the opposite: in man the quality of woman, in woman the spirit of man; in the sun, the form of the moon, in the moon the light of the sun. The closer one approaches reality, the nearer one arrives at unity.

✷ The evidence of this is shown when no sooner has a question arisen in your heart, than the answer comes as its echo, within or without. If we look before ourselves, the answer is before us; if we look behind, the answer is behind; if we look up the answer awaits us in the sky; if we look down, the answer is engraved for us in the earth; if we close our eyes we will find the answer within us. It is only a matter of climbing a mountain; and the name of this mountain is 'why'.

✷ As a child we begin the process of distrusting our intuition, relying on others for our answers. Re-learning to trust confidently in our self and what we are capable of actually doing for ourselves, also demands that we listen to our self both with consistency and sincerity. Those rare times when we have been able to be sincerely honest with our self remind us once more that regardless of the question facing us, the answer lies within us.

✷ We always know the answer, but only by learning to have faith in that answer, irrespective of what risk we might perceive in it, will we hear it with clarity. Such is the paradox of any gifted power, that unless we declare our faith in it by heeding its guidance, it will not perform.

𐐒 There is no lock, or even door, to this superconscious energy that willingly delivers abundant creativity, inspiration and guidance. The only requirement is to be aware of and receptive to its flow. By shifting our attention when we feel this flow, we consciously cast our line into its depths. Such certainty will always hook the right answer.

LESSON

11

Kissing the Scorpion

Following Your True Nature

'*Y*ou must ask yourself why you behave as you do in order to stop wasting your natural forces,' said Yen Tzu to Merchant Wong.

'But I do get nervous over forthcoming events. How should I act when attending them?' continued to ask the pupil.

'There was once a scorpion,' began the Patriarch in answer, 'who, in desiring to cross a river, asked a duck to ferry him over on her back. The duck replied that if it were to do such a foolish thing, the scorpion would undoubtedly kill her with a lethal sting.

'That's nonsense,' the scorpion argued, 'for if I did, what would save me from drowning? You have my most solemn word and sincere promise that I will not repay your kindness with such an act.'

Allowing herself to be persuaded by the scorpion's entreaties, the duck permitted the scorpion to climb on her back. But they were only halfway across the river when she felt the cruel sting of the scorpion's tail. Immediately paralysed with just a few seconds to live, the duck asked why it was that, despite his word and causing his own imminent death, the scorpion had stung her. Just before the scorpion itself fell into the rushing waters, he answered the duck, saying that he had had no choice. He was following a scorpion's true nature.'

'So am I to act like the scorpion?' exclaimed the merchant. 'But that means being ruthless, which is not in my nature.'

'It is not a matter of being ruthless or compassionate,' said Yen Tzu. 'It is a matter of acting as you are. The duck was persuaded to follow a false nature. Its true nature was clearly to not let its arch enemy onto its vulnerable back, but it allowed its false nature to dominate.

'In the mineral kingdom, diamonds are diamonds and gold is gold wherever they are placed,' continued the Patriarch, 'yet for each there exists a false copy that serves to confuse seekers. For the true nature of each is disguised and seldom recognised in rough form unless the seeker is both knowledgeable and looking.

'Yet the true form of all precious substances is more recognisable because it has undergone a process to become finer and finer until the refined spirit of the rock radiates its beauty. For, in truth, all matter is dense spirit, and spirit is finer matter. In the animal kingdom a dog is a dog and behaves as such because it's obliged to be what it is whatever the outcome. It is indifferent to whether it is rising or falling in the scale of things, to whether it is multiplying or becoming extinct.

'All mineral, vegetable and animal matter obey the law of their species, bowing their head under the yoke in which the wisdom of God imposes. For them there is no evil or sin as in our meanings of the words. There is no need for psychological effort, for their species is fixed. Man, however, can be, on occasion, as frightened as a mouse, as loyal as a dog, as brave as a lion, or as lethal as a scorpion.

'Man is the sliding note in the scale. This note is precarious; it is a state of responsibility, an octave in which Man can go up the scale or down. As Man occupies so many parts of a sliding scale, human nature is a mixture of good and evil, compassion and thoughtlessness, assist and sting. When his effort is to be himself, he can slide up the scale; when his effort is not, he can just as well slide down and degenerate.

'We can never know how to act correctly as long as we live with a mind filled with false ideas about ourselves. Following our true nature requires overcoming the wall that our false thinking has constructed to bar our way. The wall must be scaled with personal effort, for that is the test of our sincerity.'

'But after the wall is scaled,' asked the merchant, 'how is the right path to take known?'

'Because there is a growing sense of familiarity and closeness about everything when we are following our true path,' said Yen Tzu. 'And as we gradually come closer to what is our real home, we recognise it.'

✙ It is far easier to feel comfortable when we are at home, because we know where everything is. Both our essential and changing needs are supplied far more conveniently than when we are away. Similarly, we will feel uncomfortable when absent from our *psychic* home, because our true needs are not met. When our true needs are not supplied we seek to fill the void with alternatives. Based on our false beliefs as to what we think will fulfil us, they instead leave us feeling as though something is missing. That is why so many people have a feeling of emptiness in their lives, where instead there should be fullness.

¥ The way we presently behave is the only way we can, because our behaviour is determined by our psychic level. We cannot act above that level, for we are that level. But it is possible to raise our level, indeed it is our *nature* to do so. In understanding that all things behave according to their nature we can learn to see things as they should be. It requires clearing our minds of whatever has no right to be there, in order to have a clear path home. But it is here we hit a fundamental difficulty. For it is often the weight of our responsibilities that block our way.

¥ Paradoxically, the more we become conscious of our responsibilities, the less we are able to recognise the power of wisdom which is already available to us. We can become so busy meeting with what we consider our responsibilities, that we have little time to pursue our true path, by far our most important responsibility. Subsequently, we are forced into the ruts of mediocre thinking of getting by and being average.

¥ The question we might well ask ourselves later in life is: 'Why did we spend so much of our time doing things which proved of little value, yet seemed so important?' But the question each of us will surely have to answer soon after is: 'Why were you not simply yourself?' Suddenly excuses such as: 'Because there was never enough time', will become meaningless. We must not learn too late the pointlessness of stating reasons for why we didn't become what we were intended to become, or why we expressed ourselves through what we allowed others to impress upon us, rather than from our true nature.

✴ When we do things in a new way, we live differently. We bring no benefits to ourselves until we see something about ourselves that we have not seen before. A person can be told countless times to change their ways, but nothing will happen until they tell themselves the very same thing.

✴ Unfortunately this usually happens when the pain they are experiencing causes them to exchange their mistaken path for their true one. It seems to take suffering and adversity before many people are led to express their true nature, but it doesn't have to. It is important to believe that there is another way to do things, our own particular way.

✴ Developing our own path requires having the courage and tenacity to live according to three keys - spontaneous non-conformity, volitional responsibility and vocational balance.

Spontaneous Non-Conformity

An ailing Emperor grew worse despite the efforts of all the court physicians. The court fool suggested that his master might try a physician-sage who had healing powers.

Hearing this, the Emperor's personal physicians laughed. 'It takes a fool to know one!' they advised. *'We do not recognise this sage, as a physician at all,'* they added derogatorily. In his desperation, however, the Emperor was prepared to try anything and summoned the sage, who refused to attend him. Infuriated the Emperor sent a platoon of guards to seize the impudent physician-sage and bring him to the palace.

'I have brought you here because I am suffering from a strange paralysis,' said the Emperor. *'If you cure me, I will reward you. If not, I will kill you.'*

The physician-sage replied, *'In order to treat you, I need complete privacy.'* So the Emperor sent everybody out of the room, although the haughty court physicians tried to insist that they be allowed to observe. The sage waited as, eyeing his uncourtly apparel disdainfully, they were led out of the room. When the door was shut the sage took out a knife and slowly beginning to advance toward the Emperor said, *'Now I shall take my revenge for you threatening me!'*

Terrified, the invalid jumped up and ran around the room, forgetting his paralysis in his need to escape from the seemingly crazed physician.

Hearing his cries the guards rushed in, followed by all the physicians, advisors and the court fool. *'He tried to murder me!'* exclaimed the Emperor, not actually realising that he had been cured by the such an effective method.

The guards were busy ordering, the advisors looking disapprovingly at the sage, and the physicians were busy consoling, while all were trying to robe him. The Emperor continued to stamp up and down in outrage and fear.

'How wonderful to see you up and about again!' shouted the fool above the mêlée. *'You're cured!'*

✷ Whoever chooses to be their self must be a non-conformist. The successful leader, the executive, the innovator, is always the exceptional person. That person is not a conformist, except in his or her adherence to their own ideals and beliefs. Society expects, however, that we conform to a particular way of thinking, that we should act through external consideration rather than through some inner spontaneity. And to what cost do we surrender our individual character by imitating and thus being conditioned by society, which acts in the name of knowing what is best for the individual? Each time we conform to the opinion of others we blur the impressions of our own character.

✷ No-one achieves the lasting rewards of success by being a conformist. Yet many people adhere rigidly to patterns they believe some nebulous majority has decreed are prerequisites for approval for success. In this, they fall prey to a fundamental fallacy – the belief that the majority is automatically and invariably right. Yet the majority is by no means omniscient just because it is the majority. In truth, the line dividing majority and mass hysteria can be virtually invisible. If the majority of people think one particular thing it hardly guarantees the validity of opinion. More innovative success has been spawned by people uninfluenced by opinion, than by strict adherence to the accepted process.

✷ The conformist is not born, he or she is made. Indeed, the incessant pressures that bombard individuals, in order that they can be permitted to climb the ladder of acceptance towards success, come from all sides, only differing slightly from generation to generation: 'Yes, you can rebel, but the time will come when you will have to make your own way, and that way must be the established way.' In wanting to achieve success and wealth, young individuals already brainwashed on how they should ensure their security, will adopt the clothes and manner of what is considered to be the successful stereotype. The truth is that we go where we hope to go, and further, when we give up trying to look and act like everyone else.

� Being a non-conformist and acting from a natural spontaneity will get us where we want to go. Spontaneity should not to be confused with impulsiveness. The former is a voluntary action without external incitement; the latter is the tendency to act suddenly without reflection, because of external influence. The individual who can think and act independently allows their originality, imagination, self-reliance and resourcefulness to develop.

✣ The truly successful person maintains their individuality, even though their behaviour may be frowned upon by others. All the 'shoulds' and 'shouldnots' of conformity repress the individual's feelings of what is right for them. Each person has their own worth and cause and must not be timid and apologetic for following their own path.

✣ So often we dismiss our own brilliant ideas and thoughts simply because they are our own, and instead favour the expression of society. And from where does society gain the expression? From a past non-conformist individual who is no longer alive to threaten the status quo. All great individuals who follow their hearts are always initially misunderstood, even maligned, before being applauded and leaving their mark. They are guided by what they feel in their hearts is right, not what is right for society.

✄ The leaders and achievers of an innovative and information hungry business world must strive to be non-conformist. But to be unconventional simply for the sake of non-conformity is not what it is about. Those who dress and eat differently to others simply to be noticed are only conforming to the rebelliousness accepted by society. The true non-conformist dresses and behaves either unconventionally or conventionally because that is how they feel comfortable. That is the way they are. It is not to get noticed, be different or labelled rebellious. It is just them. Being a non-conformist is having the courage to say 'no' to something because it conflicts with his or her own path; even if the majority would give their eye teeth to say 'yes' for the same thing.

✄ The individual at work, who crosses swords with his or her superiors, may sometimes risk his or her job in the process. But a business that will fire someone merely because they have the courage of their convictions is not the place a person true to themselves would want to work. Any place where people are afraid to say what they believe, make mistakes, or be radically innovative in the interests of the company, will only be successful in developing seasoned conformists. A place where the established status quo must be rigidly preserved.

⅄ A good gauge to measure whether we are being true to our nature in this respect is to become aware of how we are with others. Getting jaw ache through displaying a forced smile in company when we do not feel at ease, or in answer to conversation that does not interest us, is conforming. The unspontaneous muscles which become uncomfortable to us are the physical manifestation of the discomfort which we experience through being what we feel we should be. The inner sensation we experience dissipates our inner energy, which is strong only when we are being our own person.

⅄ It is through our spontaneity that we can guide ourselves back to following our true nature; as it is a measure of how much we are internally driven, as opposed to externally influenced. Anything is right if it is a correct expression of spontaneity. Unfortunately, many people have lost their natural spontaneity as a result of living amid the contention and rivalry of our conformist-driven society.

⅄ The degree that we are externally influenced is in direct proportion to our conformism. To worry and fret about things that are superficial and trivial, even down to wearing what is considered the right clothes and living in the appropriate dwelling, is to cocoon ourselves in the culture of what others consider is best for us. To unquestionably copy those who follow the artificial path that we have been persuaded to think is the only one, is to abandon our natural path and our individuality. When we relinquish our individuality and identity of our own volition, we are effectively relinquishing our claim to being human.

✦ People who follow their own path, relying on their own intuition, above the tuition of others, inevitably stand out from the crowd. He or she finds all the doors, which they were told would be closed, opening. Society in turn solicitously, and apologetically, celebrates the individual because he or she kept to their path, choosing to ignore the disdainful and disapproving comments from the wayside. Often, it seems to take a 'fool' to shout the benefits of an individual's action, as the 'wise' are more interested in what the Emperor is wearing.

Volitional Responsibility

'But you don't even like the work you have to do!' exclaimed Kan Dou to his cousin, Wong. 'And in truth have been absent these past three years. You have always told me that you are not interested, so why do you insist on running your father's business now that Manager Ti-Lu is ill?'

'It's very simple Kan! I am the oldest, and his son, so the role of responsibility must fall to me,' argued Wong. 'Anyway, it is his wish.'

Trademaster Yen, overhearing the heated exchange between his old friend's nephew and son, later asked his friend, 'By my ancestors those two boys fight! With Ti-Lu so ill, is it wise to have them working together?'

'My friend,' replied the old man, 'you know that it has been my dream that my number one son, Wong, enters the business. With Ti-Lu away this is a golden opportunity. Anyway, nephew Kan's understanding of the business is excellent. Having worked

at the House of Dou since a child he knows it better than me, or Ti-Lu. If there is any problem, he will be able to guide his elder cousin.'

'Forgive me, but the question, as to why you do not simply allow Kan responsibility, arises in me,' said Trademaster Yen.

'Because I can already depend on Kan,' came back the answer from his friend. 'But I am hoping that in holding a position of such responsible and power, my first born will be persuaded to return to the Dou Trading House.'

'Let us hope that he respects the order of such factors,' said Trademaster Yen. 'For without the temperance of the former, the latter runs out of control. The burden of duty comes before its rewards. I trust all turns out well for you old friend.'

Returning from a six-month trip to Chao Province, Trademaster Yen was not surprised to learn of the near demise of the old house of Dou. More interested in the respectability of his position than his duties, his old friend's eldest son had indulged himself using the security of the House of Dou's bonds. The anticipated order from a long-standing client had been cancelled because the irresponsible Wong, ignoring Kan, had caused the client to lose face.

'But it is not my fault,' argued Wong, glancing at Kan begrudgingly. 'If Kan had ratified the order, there would have been no losing of face!'

'To make a mistake is one thing, but to blame your cousin is another,' said his father. 'You knew it was your responsibility to deal with Heads of House, because you are the appointed Head of House! There would have been loss of face if you had not gone. But how could you commit our bonds?'

'What else could you expect,' said Wong. 'You are to blame

father, not I, for how could you expect me to gain the respect of everyone since my return without the trappings of my position?'

✝ Perhaps the most important 'R' we should be taught at school before those of reading, writing and arithmetic is the understanding of responsibility. Through our formative years we are taught the ability to react, rather than the ability to respond, so our tendency is to follow the philosophy of: 'It's not a matter of win or lose, it's where we place the blame.' This in turn leads to our willingness to fight for the credit when good things happen, and our unwillingness to accept responsibility for our actions when bad things happen.

✝ This unnatural culture is misguidedly based on the desire to seek early gratification, to minimise risk and to ensure security by making others responsible for the quality of our lives. Paradoxically, we seek to increase our success, while wanting those who we have voted to govern to provide us with more financial security; we demand less interference in our social habits, while pleading for more protection from crime; and we fight for more authority over decisions that effect us, while accepting less responsibility for the outcome. The simple fact is, however, that life's greatest risk is to depend on others for our security.

✝ Only by individually taking full responsibility for what our life is and is not, in *every* way, are we capable of developing our inherent powers. Only then do we feel secure and develop our ability to respond to risk effectively, regardless of what happens. Whenever we blame others for our life situations, we shift our power to those whom we believe are responsible for creating the circumstances.

✦ Being fully responsible means to view everything that happens to us from the position that there are absolutely no accidents in our lives, and that everything that occurs has a lesson attached to it that we bring upon ourselves. This means accepting that, however absurd something is, our own thought energies have created it; we do actually bring upon ourselves everything uncomfortable that happens to us. When we are able to accept this, we allow our sense of responsibility to grow. In turn it becomes impossible to blame another for either minor problems or major disappointments in our lives.

✦ With entrenched and firmly established mental and emotional frames of reference, ensuring we are not at fault when something happens to us, it is of course hard to change. Indeed the plethora of work attributed by the law profession and insurance stand testimony to this. Yet metaphysically we always relinquish our personal power when we seek to attribute blame or evade responsibility. For this reason, it is infinitely better to ensure that whatever we get involved with or do is from our own volition.

✦ How responsible we choose to be towards what we do is relative to how much we love, are effective, and excel in what we do. Whether we do things of our own volition or not, we must always take responsibility for our actions. But it is indeed far easier when we do what we are doing because we want to. Developing volitional responsibility means reinventing ourselves to become permanently self-employed team players. This means that we are each our own chairman of the board and managing director, with a lifetime contract to operate our own service company with a single employee.

✻ To hold such a position requires us to set an example in our own lives. It means being proactive, instead of reactive. Metaphorically it involves investing both time and energy in our own personal research and development centre; establishing our own strategic planning division; setting up a human resource department to make sure that our top employee receives continuous training initiatives; starting our own pension provisions and, of course, providing both customer relationship and quality control centres.

✻ Being responsible for our future requires determining a vision and communicating it to our main employee; ascertaining our viability in our industry and thinking strategically. To embrace such responsibility of our own volition means it is not possible to apportion blame, because such action is instantly recognised as pointless. Indeed, each time our work sparks insecurity and the need to either blame or take credit arises we must ask ourselves if what we are doing is what we really want to do.

✻ Volitional responsibility allows ready acknowledgement that even though there are things in life beyond our control;

we naturally have control over our responses. We have, for example, control over our attitude, our tongue, our promises, our energy, our imagination and our choices. What we choose to do with our free time is within our control. Who we choose to have relationships with, to mentor us, to influence us and to either judge, mock or unkindly criticise us, is also within our control.

✝ We can control our concerns, worries and actions in the knowledge that it is not any single event that has control over us; rather it is only our estimation of the event that we allow to affect us. And this estimate relates to how much our natural ability to cope is in control, or how much our unnatural reluctance prevails. This in turn leads to the state of balance in our lives.

Vocational Balance

'This will be ideal for my meditations,' thought a wandering sage, seeking a cave in the wilderness. Upon entering it, however, he noticed the skeletal remains of many human corpses. Unconcerned, he sat down on a rock to rest from his travels.

'How you answer will seal your fate!' boomed a voice, and turning the sage saw that before him was a gigantic scorpion, the size of a large man.

'As your questions have undoubtedly sealed yours,' replied the sage calmly.

'What manner of Man are you to be without trace of fear?' demanded the giant scorpion. 'For the nature of Man is to be afraid.'

'Not so,' answered the sage. 'For in truth the nature of Man is to be in balance, and such a state comes when he has no fear of what life may confront him with, because he is in love with the true meaning of life. As my thoughts and actions have led me to this place, how can I fear it? To do so is to fear myself, which I do not, for I have only love for the person that I am.'

'Then you are rare indeed,' said the scorpion, 'for the men who have come before you have been escaping from themselves, as one seeks to leave another within a loveless relationship.'

'You speak as one who has experienced such,' said the sage intuitively, 'for your visage is not strong enough to hide the pain, frustration and indeed anger that you exude.'

'It would seem that truthful perception is yours to command,' answered the fearsome creature. 'Because in truth I was as a man once, long ago, until my ruthlessness attracted a demon seeking a disciple. My resistance to it resulted in having my current condition cast upon me. But because what was left of my original nature was able to resist, the demon was compelled to allow my situation a reversal. Though little use it has been. For of all those who have approached my lair these past long years, none have caused the spell to be reversed.'

'Because no doubt they must answer of their own accord and without direction,' said the sage. 'An accord distorted by their fear.'

'Exactly so! And now you will forgive me if I become impatient to address the riddle I must ask of you!' said the scorpion. 'If you refuse to answer, cannot or your answer is wrong, then I thank you in advance for our debate, for afterwards it will be too late.'

'Proceed as you wish,' the sage said, 'for it is of little consequence.'

'Take heed though,' advised the scorpion 'that immediately after I have incanted my words I will be rendered helpless in order to allow you to make your choice. Although you are weaponless, there are many swords around you that are sharp enough to enable even the weakest of arms to slice off my deadly tail. And so:

'When you embrace the most deadly, you overcome your worst fears;
When you act the least likely, there can be nothing but tears;
When you act from the heart and engage worthy might,
Then to the end from the start, you have held to what's right;
Your balance to death will be as it is for your life,
To do one over the other, can bring sorrow and strife;
When you act as you do because you are as you be,
You will know if a kiss or a strike is the key.

'Quickly!' added the now motionless scorpion looking menacingly into the eyes of the sage. 'You have the opportunity to strike me.'

'My answer is as my action,' said the sage and calmly outstretched his arms and kissed the creature on its evil-looking head. Immediately the scorpion was transformed and it was now a man that stood before him. With the spell broken, tears flowed freely down the large man's cheeks and he fell at the feet of the sage in gratitude. As the sage helped him up, the large man said, 'You chose correctly, yet why were you so sure, when the nature of a scorpion is to strike when face to face with its adversary?'

'Because deep down you were still a man,' said the sage, 'and it is the true-nature of a man to love, not strike. And as the riddle implied, transforming you back into a man is the greatest risk to overcome, because Man can be more deadly than any scorpion. Acting in the least likely way of not seemingly protecting myself could only release your tears. Those tears a man has prior to his transformation and the tears of happiness that follow it. Furthermore because I am in a state of balance I can but only act in a right manner.'

'I am indeed fortunate to have found such a natural individual to release me from my predicament,' said the man.

'Fortune has nothing to do with it,' replied the sage with finality. 'It was your own need to return to your true vocation that attracted you to me, and it was my own thoughts to test my own vocation that led me to you. All of us are interdependent of others whether we are aware of it or not. As such, all of us are both teachers and students, appearing as appropriate to one another when each is ready. That is how we can fulfil our true vocation. Learning how to express it effectively requires a state of balance. For only in such a state can we act as our true nature intended.'

✦ Instead of being frightened by life's conditions it is important to address them calmly, to meet our conditions with understanding, self-forgiveness and love, rather than resignation. Each of us has the power to be master of our life by following our own particular nature. The truth is that nothing is Man's nature except that which he makes for himself. Of all creation, Man is the most entitled to be optimistic, yet prefers the artificial nature of pessimism.

✆ Optimism represents a spontaneous flow of love, trust and an attitude of hopefulness. Pessimism comes from disappointment, from a bad impression formed from some hindrance of the past. Perhaps pessimism may show conscientiousness and experience, but can we be in balance if our tendency is to think only of what difficulties may lay ahead of us? The psychological effect of optimism is such that it helps towards success – surely it was by the optimistic spirit that all creation was born - whereas pessimism is born out of the mind of man.

✆ For the optimistic individual it does not matter if things do not come out just right, they will take their chance, for Life is an opportunity and as such should be seized, not withdrawn from. There are many people, however, who prolong their condition, either in illness or poverty, by nurturing it with pessimistic thoughts. They can unwittingly do so until the condition becomes so real that absence of it seems unnatural. They believe that the state that they experience is their nature, that their misery is their share in life, that they are born to be wretched and cannot be anything else but unhappy.

✆ An optimist will naturally help another who is drowning in fear or disappointment. A pessimist, conversely, upon meeting such a person will sink them even further into their despair. So on the one side is the kiss of life, on the other the sting of death. The former is natural; the latter is referred to as being realistic. But the only reality is that Infinite Spirit comes to Man's rescue in the form of optimism. It does not matter how difficult a situation in life we face; all can be surmounted. What does matter is that we balance the scales of our heart with greater optimism, as the weight of a pessimistic spirit is so much heavier.

✻ It is when we are tired enough, or when the pain of our situation is intense enough, that we will seek change. The change we must seek to re-vitalise ourselves requires re-balancing the scales of what each of us finds natural to do, against that which we have the responsibility to do.

✻ The measurement for finding and achieving a natural balance through what we do, is how optimistic we feel when we are expressing what we do. We must ask ourselves on a regular basis how enthusiastic we feel about our work, the very expression of our vocation. If the answer is that we are not, then we must take that as a clear signal that our lives are out of vocational balance.

✻ Optimism and enthusiasm go hand in hand because they both emanate from a spiritual source; one feeds the other. It is not possible to be enthusiastically pessimistic. We can achieve much more in our lives when we are in balance, so it is important to generate enthusiasm wherever it is lacking. Enthusiasm of course differs from person to person, but everyone can recognise when another has it. He or she enjoys and believes in what they do, and their conviction is infectious. Something springs from within them and seems natural. We are magically drawn towards the natural, whether it is a scene in nature, a moment of sincerity between two people, or a person who exudes natural enthusiasm. We are attracted because we know without being told that the natural is the right.

𝑌 Unfortunately, we are not so capable of noticing it, or its lack, in ourselves, and furthermore may even have the tendency to sting such positivity in others. We burst the bubble of another when in our opinion their head is too much in the clouds, and they ought to be brought back down to earth. We catch ourselves saying something to our child, that was once unthoughtfully said to us, and which we were certain we would never say ourselves. The fact is that the excitement a child feels is natural, as is the nervous anticipation and excitement that a new employee feels when first commencing work. Do any of us have the right to dampen that natural enthusiasm? Not at all, but everyday, it is done in countless families and offices in the name of reality.

𝑌 Each of us has a responsibility to ourselves to constantly monitor our transformation. Deep down inside each of us rest our inherent scales, which easily tell us when we are out of balance. We have but to listen to them by gauging how we feel at certain times. If everyday we wake up and go about our business robotically, without enjoyment, then we are certainly not in balance with what we do.

✔ We must ask ourselves if we are following our true vocation, and courageously embrace the answer. If we are not, then our personal transformation will most likely start when we acknowledge the right answer and take action. If we are, then we can examine if we are allowing distraction to veer us off our true path. When we enjoy vocational balance we are following our true nature, as we are in tune with what we do and what we do is an expression of what we are. We are in command of life when we are at one with it.

Unified Diversity

✔ The common theme of ancient wisdom, irrespective of time and culture, has always been to return and follow our original and true nature. The difference between artificiality and naturalness in our lives can be likened to an earnest actor. Using memorised lines and practiced gestures, he is able to convince the audience that he is true to the false role he is performing. After the departure of the audience, however, he is able to be himself once more. There is no longer a contradiction between his true-self and acted role. Yet, were he to take the part continuously, a blur between the two identities would result, until the acted, more familiar role, dominated. Although his original nature would always exist it would remain dormant.

✔ Wherever there exists a well-established artificial nature, disunity within that person is inevitable. With disunity comes tension and strained attempts to control our lives which, paradoxically, actually cause lack of control. To be unified means to be harmoniously at one with ourself. The true nature of two individuals may be as diverse as chalk and cheese, as each individual is unique. But whenever we follow our true nature we are automatically in tune with the natural flow of life.

✙ That is the miracle of life, that in our unified diversity we can each learn to become our own person, fulfilling our own potential and realising our own special meaning and purpose. Yet in following our true nature, we help fulfil the well-intentioned aspirations of those whose paths cross ours, because of our very connectedness with them.

✙ Learning to live with natural spontaneity, acknowledging responsibility in all our personal and interpersonal choices, and seeking balance in how we express ourselves, will unerringly guide us back to our original nature. We have the capability and potential without doubt, but ultimately it is up to each of us, as individuals, to stop blocking our natural path. Transformation from the artificial role that we act, into the natural person we are, means doing just that.

If you could get rid
Of yourself just once,
The secret of secrets
Would open to you.
The face of the unknown,
Hidden beyond the universe
Would appear on the
Mirror of your perception.

Rumi

Awaiting the Turtle

Being in the Right Place at the Right Time

'The opportunity for Human Life is rare,' began the Patriarch, Yen Tzu. 'So rare that it can be likened to that magical event which occurs just once every four hundred years. The moment when the great mythical sea turtle rises for air. Imagine, that while breaking the surface, the creature places its head through a bamboo ring. A hoop that happens to be floating randomly alone in the vast ocean. What perfect timing that would take! Imagine too that this solitary wooden necklace fitted exactly. What precision that would be! Now imagine that the human physical body is the bamboo circle, and the turtle is the immortal spirit entering it. Then you can imagine the perfect coming together of forces that must happen for our own birth.'

'It is indeed hard to consider that our life is such a rarity,' replied his pupil, Lu Chou. 'Just look at the countless people going about their business in the Imperial city each day!'

'Just so,' answered Yen Tzu, 'and each one of them is just where they should be. For in truth our lives are the result of a synchronicity between the physical and spiritual. As such, each one of us began our lives at the rightly appointed time, and in the correct place intended.'

'That must be why one person's timing in life seems infinitely better than another's,' commented Lu Chou. 'Where one man seems to make his fortune, another does not; where one struggles to no avail, another seems to attain easily.'

'That is not the reason,' said the Patriarch, 'for the time and place has nothing to do with a man's success. The rightness and timing in awaiting the turtle is merely to illustrate that such synchronicity is our birthright. But Man, instead of resolving to continue to use this natural serendipitous power, has become conditioned do the opposite.

'In doing so he unconsciously acts against himself, seeking to manipulate and control outcomes according to his own rules. He has forgotten that everything that is to happen for his benefit does so at the right time; and everything that is forced beyond a natural course of events is either lost or distorted.

'Even if the outcome is seemingly right it does not carry the power it would have had, or bring the benefit it was intended to bring. The result is that the harder he seems to push towards that which he wants, the further it moves away from him. Such is the plight of all who take the heritage of how they came to be for granted. Yet, in truth, knowing how to harness our natural synchronicity with Life's opportunities creates the paradox of the less we do, the more we achieve.'

'So what can we do to regain this power, this heritage,' asked the pupil.

'We must steadfastly resolve to live, trust, accept and have purpose in whatever we do, at the moment we are doing it. For *the nature of being always in the right place at the right time is ours to command.'*

✝ Resolving to change something in our lives requires us to let go of something. Yet, in so doing, we gain considerably more. A steadfast resolve does not mean making those frequent shallow resolutions we often indulge in, for they soon flounder and drown as soon as familiar old habits regain command over our intent. True resolve is both rare and sincere and is only made more profound by being tested in the worst circumstances over a period of time. Regardless of the duration of the period, it is, upon reflection, always timely, and provides the opportunity to express our stronger, true-self.

✝ Our resolve is the measure of our commitment to that which we know is important to us. Without knowledge of our own unique what, why and wherefore, earnest resolve is neither forthcoming, nor will endure when the obstacles inevitably encountered become too great. Consequently, when we seek security from something outside of ourselves, we join the rollercoaster of life; one which promises excitement when things go right, but also the risk of significant lows when they don't.

✝ Whenever we allow others control over the start and stop buttons of our life this further develops the false sense of self first spawned through our formative years. This leads to false desires and subsequently false activities, and, in turn, to false problems and false sufferings. The result is that we are continually out of sync with our true selves.

✝ Regaining our natural synchronicity in the order of things is vital to every area of our lives. Whatever our situation or circumstance; it is where our current level of thinking has placed us. Quite simply, our thinking has manifested what our sense of self deems appropriate. It follows, therefore, that a true or false sense of self will align us with the opportune or inopportune accordingly.

✝ At birth we were fine, and then well-meaning others unwittingly sought to define us for the best. It is now important to refine ourselves in order to harness the abundance and opportunity specifically awaiting us. To re-learn the secret of being in the right place at the right time requires understanding and application of the following practices.

Living in the Moment

'Let us recall the tale of Chen Su-Lee, the famous turtle catcher', continued Yen Tzu, 'who ended up being caught himself. It was at a time when he was enjoying a lazy swim in familiar waters after a long and successful day's fishing. Suddenly he intuitively became aware of something following him. Turning he saw what he knew to be a lethal giant eel and immediately sought to escape.

'Despite his strong strokes, his resourceful heart began to

despair, for he knew that the water ahead held stronger currents and his strength was depleting. With adrenaline coursing rapidly through his veins, he was able to reach a small rock in the nick of time. Resting just above the surface it would provide safety from the deadly eel. Safe at last he thought! Quickly he scrambled upon it and lay flat and still.

'He had only been there for a matter of moments when the awful realisation came to him that he was sharing his sanctuary with a sleeping venomous water viper. One bite from its evil mouth would bring his death instantaneously. No matter, thought the catcher, I will stay here until that monster eel has gone, and hope this viper continues its dreams. But, hearing a screeching noise above him he looked up to see two gulls swooping down to land upon his resting place. His impending doom seemed certain, as already the viper had become aware of the disturbance. At that moment he noticed a half-open oyster shell and, ignoring his imminent fate, he plucked the most magnificent white pearl from within it and enjoyed its splendid beauty as it sat in the palm of his hand.

'You see,' concluded Yen Tzu, 'There was little point in feeling unhappy about how he happened to be in this situation. A catcher for most of his life, he had used all his experience to escape, so why waste his precious last few moments fretting over the future. Admittedly he had not taken the usual care recently, but what was past was history and all the hoping in the world would not change previous actions.

'The present moment, the very here and now is the time to experience and cherish the fullness of what life offers. This is all any of us have at any one time. That moment must have our full attention.'

151

Yen Tzu

✝ When our life is supremely concentrated in the present, there is no need to worry about what has been, or be fearful for what may be. For the right response will come to us for every situation as it occurs. That is our real freedom; the ability to enjoy the choices we make in every successive moment of the present.

✝ Very few people are able to live in the present moment of their lives. Whether in relationships or business, they allow their lives to be directed by past or future influences. Most choices are made under the rational mind that prompts, 'bearing in mind the circumstances, this is the most appropriate decision.' By letting go of all influences we are able to feel intuitively which direction we want to take, regardless of the circumstances.

Man-Ho Ping was a great but unhappy merchant. Leader of a group of businesses trading in sixteen provinces, he employed 10,000 people. Over the years the culture of his business had radically changed from one of harmony to one of defence and blame. On a rare visit to a local tea emporium he found himself next to his old friend Honest Lo.

'You look well old friend,' he declared in delight.

'I wish I could say the same of you Merchant Ping,' replied Honest Lo. 'For my eyes see a weariness and concern.'

'Indeed, I admit your eyes are correct. I believe that my ability to delegate has been the reason for my success, but the select team I have chosen to diligently train over the years are not performing as I had hoped. They have become focused only

on results, which is what I had wanted so that I could measure my growth. But the atmosphere is so tense when I am around them. What has happened? What should I do? These are the questions that give me my present expression.'

'Ah,' pondered Lo. 'In my experience of business and relationships, indeed any situation where there is interaction of thought, I believe that silence communicates more. Where is the usefulness of the pot, the external feature or the emptiness inside? More is communicated by the empty space circled by a group of people than what is actually spoken from the circle. The emptiness tells you how things are.'

'Well the emptiness is not good,' agreed Ping. 'But how do I change it?'

'In training your team to become focused on results, you have moved away from the natural course of the way things operate. For, though a river seeks to meet the ocean, it has no control over when. And though it is the nature of the acorn to grow, it has no control as to whether it will be successful. Power only exists over processes, not results.

'So, always remember, in delegating responsibility one must also give the power to go with it. Having your people work on the process gives them the power needed to fill the emptiness of their former responsibility.'

☙ With the focus of attention on results, the influence over process becomes weak. Systems break down and energy is then directed in damage limitation through defence and blame. In the early days of a business, for example, the focus is clearly on the strengths that participants are able to bring to it. When these strengths are channelled into the daily process of what is best for growth, benefits in the form of increased productivity naturally result. This is similar to water in a river. Through its flow of focus and energy, it persistently seeks the path of least resistance rather than the shortest route. Consistently increasing in strength and substance, it always reaches its objective, the ocean, which, in turn, replenishes the rivers source.

✣ Once a business has matured, however, it seems to realign its focus of attention from strengths to weaknesses. It becomes like an enclosed canal, seeking to shore up weak banks which distract it from the shortest route required to maintain growth. Containing and protecting its position like a huge dam, it inevitably loses its fluidity. When the incoming river of new ideas and energy dries up there is little concern, for what does it matter when we already have such a reservoir?

✣ Yet water that is no longer fluid becomes stagnant. Too many organisations unwittingly illustrate to their detriment, a reservoir culture. When natural flow is impeded, making headway becomes harder and the timing of opportunities is lost. Customers who rely on service, for example, will soon form an opinion as to the culture of a company.

✣ No-one has control over the results in their lives. On first encounter this precept is difficult to accept. The practice of manipulating the future forms the basis of most strategies in our modern world. This is coupled with the practice of planning a future on an expected outcome, rather than being one hundred percent aware of what is happening right where you are – the very here and now.

✴ The man wanting to date a woman he really likes, for example, does not live in the present moment. First he is thinking of what she will say when he asks her for a date. Should her answer be yes, much of his 'here and now' is occupied thinking of the future event. Thoughts of the actual date occupy the days leading up to it. Thoughts of what may happen after dinner occupy the time spent eating dinner. Each present moment experience is lost as the mind is anticipating the future. If at the moment of the date, unforeseen circumstances cause her to change her mind, the man has missed out on much more than an event. He has missed the experience of all those moments leading up to the date. If, on the other hand the date goes ahead but does not conclude as anticipated, the man may then dwell in the past analysing it.

✴ We are only able to influence a result by what we do in the present, because the process of our lives is only contained within our present. We therefore have control over our processes, but we do not have control over our results. Although it is wise to establish the basis of an outcome, it is important to have flexibility thinking in order to anticipate and plan.

✴ As we do not live in the future, we have no control over it. The majority of people, however, seek to make the future happen according to their wishes. The paradox being that the harder they push for something, the further it moves away. By focusing one hundred percent of their energy on what is fully under their control, which is the process of what they do from moment to moment, they gain the greatest influence possible over a desired outcome.

✯ When owners, shareholders and decision makers who form the 'top-line' of a company, for example, are bottom-line driven they become future-result-focused in their actions; rather than present-process-focused. In doing so they unwittingly put into motion those forces that actually bring about the reverse of that which they intended. Furthermore, when anticipated results do not materialise, focus is switched to what is now a *past* process.

✯ It is energy that makes things happen, and in this instance the term 'focus' refers to the level of energy. Physical form represents an outcome of energy transference; whatever is materially created must first be mentally generated. Therefore the quality of what we do is dependent on the level of energy we are able to focus with. For example, in physics, it takes the same energy to light a spotlight as it does to cut through metal with a laser; the latter is simply more focused. Metaphysically, whenever our energy is diluted, by thinking about what must happen, or what should have happened, to fulfil a result, we divert our energy away from the actual process that occupies our present. Yet it is our focusing on the present process that is the key to creating the results we desire.

✔ Seeking control over a result requires us to interfere with the process. A bird learns to fly through trial and error. With the care and attention bestowed from the parent solely focused on the present moment process, the desired result comes about.

✔ *Merchant Man-Ho Ping*, had not let go of his 'young.' He had trained his team to fly, while at the same time clipping their wings. This prevented them from putting their real hearts into flying, and instead focused their energy on vying for position within the nest. Business executives, who seek to control results according to the way they believe things should be, unwittingly move the company's energy, and the energy of those they influence, away from present process into future results. Thus the 'bird' whose clipped wings prevent further growth will ensure that its own position in the nest is kept, by adopting a 'defend and blame' stance. Such behaviour is then duplicated by others.

✔ Living in the present moment requires consciously focusing on what we are actually experiencing, rather than what we hope to experience. Understanding fully that we only have control over process and not result, leads to the requirement and application of the next practice.

Trusting in the Moment

A man travelling with a convoy of traders between provinces was greatly concerned at the talk of bandits. Spying a distinguished gentleman in a great tent some distance from the convoy he went over and said, 'Your pardon sir, but may I trust you with my purse?' Having received the gentleman's undertaking and promise to take care of the purse, the man returned to the convoy greatly relieved. But he immediately discovered that a band of thieves had robbed all the other traders during his absence.

Thanking his ancestors for his foresight, he hurried back to the gentleman's great tent to collect his purse. But he was shocked to see that the very same person, with whom he had entrusted his purse, was distributing his fellow traders' belongings amongst the band of thieves. It was the robber baron himself.

'What have I done?!' said the man. 'I have placed my wealth in the very same hand as that I sought to keep it from! Who can be more foolish than me?'

As he retreated in fear, the robber baron noticed him and called out: 'You there, what are you doing?'

Shaken, the man replied, 'I came here to retrieve my purse, but alas, I discover that I have given it into the very hands from which I wanted to keep it away.'

Looking at him intently the robber baron said: 'Please allay whatever fears you understandably have. For in truth, you are a man who put your trust in me. How can there be any question of me robbing you when you display such qualities. I gave you my word didn't I? So how can you expect me to keep your purse? Here, I now return it.'

This mutual act of trust and trustworthiness surprised some of the horde, but their leader's actions impressed many of them. It is said that in his later days the robber baron became a great teacher.

❧ By distrusting people we perhaps avoid a little loss, but the distrust that we sow in our hearts is a greater loss still. Only trustworthiness begets trust. Even when it does not, it still wins. In a materially driven world, in which a postage stamp is valued more than a word of honour because the stamp is sure, the argument is clear: 'Of course I would like to trust people, but people are not worthy of trust.' Though trusting others inevitably means that you must be ready to undergo loss, it is important not to view the world this way.

❧ It is not foolish to trust another, rather it is the wise person who trusts more than the foolish one. It is a greater strength to trust, for the one who has less trust is weak and everyday becomes weaker. The one who does not trust others will find it difficult to trust even their own family and friends, and this distrust can develop to such an extent that they do not trust themselves. This is indeed sad, for the absence of self-trust is the basis of insecurity and lack of belief in one's self.

❧ If you saw a man drowning would you shout 'I would like to save you, but I do not know you well enough to trust you yet. You might pull me down with you.' The man certainly would not shout, 'Please get someone I can trust to save me.' He is trusting in you at that moment; a moment of complete trust that both you and he will afterwards always cherish. Trusting another is testing because there is the risk of loss. Whenever another places so much trust in us we understandably re-evaluate the meaning of trust. When someone sincerely looks to us to be trustworthy, their very

159

intent begins to develop trust within us, where formerly there may have been an absence of trust.

🗲 There is the argument of course, that it is different in business. It is because of that thinking that the basic role of trust must be understood. Trust is the foundation of every strong relationship, regardless of situation or circumstance. Trust, similar to love, can be given but not necessarily received. The first person to give your trust to, therefore, is yourself. The immediate difficulty here is which you are you. When you realise the truism that your life unfolds in the way it does because 'wherever you go, you meet yourself,' then you begin to consider how you can know which of your selves the true one is.

🗲 All the great teachers have recorded that man holds false ideas about himself. Certainly it would seem that if we changed the way we thought about ourselves, we would perhaps not have the problems we think we have. The reality is that 'knowing yourself' is easier said than done, so trusting yourself can become almost impossible. Yet if you trusted yourself there would no need for second thoughts, which only serve to confuse issues. Perhaps if we experienced second thoughts first, many of our obstacles would diminish or disappear altogether.

🗲 As most of our problems spring from a lack of self-trust, rather than asking, 'What can I do about this problem?' we must learn to ask, 'What can I do to help myself?' The key to building self-trust is to go about it in the opposite way to that in which you have been taught to deal with problems. Whenever you experience a crisis, for example, take it completely on your own shoulders. Trying to share it with others immediately, in the belief that a problem shared is a problem halved, will have an adverse effect.

✻ In diluting the intensity of the problem by sharing it around, you also dilute your power for understanding and removing it. The habit of discussing our problems, whether regarding finances, human relationships, or what we should do in life, stems from not trusting and heeding our own instructive advice. When you trust in your inner guidance you rise above your problem and the answer always comes to you at the right time.

✻ Whenever you have a problem, look deeply into it. Its root will require a change in you which will in turn dissolve many other difficulties. A difficult marriage is not the issue; rather it is a false understanding of life itself and what you want from it. Difficult politics at work are not the issue; rather it is how greatly you believe that control, security, status and expectations have been compromised by the people involved.

✻ Frustration occurs when our internal demands meet external opposition. In not getting what you want your desire turns back on itself; causing you conflict. It is a false sense of self which causes those desires, for it frantically believes that its existence depends upon their fulfilment.

✸ The next time you allow yourself to experience the discomfort of what to you is a problematical situation, approach it differently. First of all, observe how your mind anxiously seeks for an answer, for relief and reassurance. Next, ask yourself if you really need the kind of answer you assume you do. Then let go of the problem's hold over you in the knowledge that you already carry the best solution within you. Finally trust in yourself by expecting the solution at the right time to resolve the problem. In this way you will unconsciously gravitate towards the solution and recognise it as such when it comes to light.

✸ Do not employ your memory to solve any inner problem that arises because of the manner in which you are addressing your external problem. Every moment of life is completely new and requires current insight. In the same way as you cannot make fire from stirring ashes, when you allow memorised action to leap into the space reserved for present consciousness, your creativity is blocked. Just try remaining quiet as you consider your next problem and see what happens. The answer may indeed come from a source outside of yourself, but you will recognise it as it will confirm what you already unconsciously know in your heart to be right.

✸ Trusting in the moment gives you great power. This must not be misunderstood as the fatalistic view of 'what will be, will be.' Far from it. Think of it instead as 'what you are, will be.' The degree to which you learn to trust yourself and your decisions is in direct proportion to the benefits you will reap at any moment. Trusting in the moment leads to the next practice.

Acceptance of the Moment

A female member of the disgraced Ling family went to visit The Old House of Ling now under the direction of the Counsellor and Empress Ni. The house was formerly under the direction of the tyrannical Prince Ling, infamous for his mercilessly critical eye. His habit of seeing the flaw in everything and everyone led to fierce rebellion in his province, resulting in his power being stripped from him.

Empress Ni was herself known as a woman of delicacy and compassion. On seeing the emaciated and ragged Princess Ling at her gate, she asked her to come in and prepared to give her words of comfort and such presents as would relieve her evident want.

But no sooner had the impoverished Princess said, 'I am a daughter of the family of Ling...' than the Empress forgot all about her charity. Her intent altered because of what she now saw before her and she shouted: 'A woman of the accursed Ling! You have come no doubt to beg for alms, forgetting what oppression your menfolk and their criticism caused to our family, how regardless of what we did we were treated without mercy, never being allowed any recourse...'

'No,' said Princess Ling, 'I did not come for sympathy, forgiveness or money. I came to see whether the family of Ni had learned from their ruthless predecessors, or whether the conduct you deplore was a contagion which would certainly end in the downfall of those who contract it.'

✦ Empress Ni allowed her natural charitable emotions to be swept aside because of emotions belonging to, and residing in, the past. In losing her present compassion in favour of past grievances, she relinquished her power over her present and future actions. By accepting the past in favour of the present, she reacted in a manner that was supposedly alien to her natural character.

✼ Often a parent is horrified to hear themselves criticising their offspring using the same admonitions they experienced so humiliatingly as a child. Many a rising executive gaining a higher position may employ criticism previously applied to his own efforts during his time as a subordinate. Both have accepted past experiences over the present and may be unconsciously prompted, through conditioned thinking, by the misconception that the best support is through what is termed 'constructive criticism'. Yet experiencing the present moment involves growing from the past, not imitating it. Feeling nervous, cynical or hard done by, for example, is caused by permitting past experiences to impose themselves upon the present moment. Yet the claim of the past upon the present is invalid.

✼ Cynicism itself, that eternal impediment to growth, is commonly wrapped up in the guise of constructive criticism. When the habit of seeking and pointing out the flaw in something, whether in presentations, opportunities, or arguments becomes endemic, the natural process is disturbed. The process of creativity, for example, is impeded when ideas being generated in a brain-storming session are evaluated at the same time.

✝ A foible unique to mankind and borne of lack of trust, cynicism prevents acceptance of process more than any other single factor. Whereas intuition stems from the facts presently at hand, cynicism relies solely on the past for its argument. Rather than seek the truth for itself, it demands to be convinced. Overcoming distrustful thinking requires encouraging involvement. As true commitment is impossible without involvement, by encouraging the cynic to be more involved in a process, rather than resisting it, he or she is allowed to embark upon the process that may result in them becoming a valued supporter.

✝ Acceptance of the moment requires acknowledging that each of us experiences a variety of rising and descending cycles. In the same way that there is a time to sow and a time to reap, a time to consolidate and a time to grow, sometimes you do well in life and other times you do not. Evidently you enjoy life more during a high cycle and do not savour the difficulties characterised by a low cycle. The key is not to become excited by the high points, or depressed by the low points. In fact, the low points are to be respected because the high is built from the low. For the *somebody* within you is built on the moments when you are *nobody*.

✝ Generally we are not taught to value the low. We are conditioned to look for high respect and exaltation. When people have a low cycle they are emotionally debilitated by it, feel terrible, and experience low self-esteem. Yet it is during these times, when they receive no attention or respect and do not love themselves, that they become wise and begin to grow. Princess Ling's character had strengthened to a point higher than Empress Ni's reputed one. Low signs, such as those we experience when nothing seems to be going our way, must be accepted as indications that we must pull back, reassess our situation, and perhaps consolidate in anticipation of that forthcoming growth cycle.

✤ During its hot cycle, nature invests abundantly in the growth that follows its cold cycle. The old is then discarded and, after a consolidation period, the new arrives. Nature accepts that you cannot grow without letting go. This natural cycle does not rest comfortably with individuals or business. Where the rare business wisely invests more than it spends in the high cycle in order that it can consolidate in a low cycle, the ordinary business will not. In good times an organisation will show the market how wonderful it is through its large budget. In difficult times, when it is important for the market to know about them, the same organisation will be forced to keep quiet by its vastly reduced budget.

✤ Although there is not one person or business that does not experience high and low cycles, few make provision. This is one of the reasons why the majority of businesses do not survive and why so many people suffer hardship during the influence of a major economic cycle. Preparing for future during the present, must not be confused with having one's consciousness in the future through worry.

✗ No-one can avoid bad cycles either in health, wealth or relationships. But if we act in the same manner as if it were a good cycle, we will reduce our discomfort. This requires us to exercise the highest performance and highest service to ourselves and those around us. Accepting the moment irrespective of its influence requires having the flexibility of the reed in the wind. It bends, and grows; it does not break.

✗ Acceptance of the moment means accepting that what is presently happening may be an indication of something we have to change. For example, a man worrying over money may actually be worrying over being labelled a loser in society's money-game. When he lets go of his false beliefs, the problem disappears. Perhaps the man's problem is being in debt through over-spending. Paying off his debts will not remove his compulsion to acquire objects in order to feel more secure.

✗ When meeting any difficulty you must ask yourself, 'Am I going to fight this or rise above it?' If you decide to fight it you will do so endlessly, for it is the very battling with the problem that keeps it going. Rise above it through using your own insight as to why you have this difficulty at the time that you do, and the problem disappears permanently. It does so because you realise that there wasn't an individual and a problem, there was only you, the individual, who was the problem. In the moments you accept to solve yourself, you solve your problem. In doing this you begin to place yourself where you are intended to be. This brings us to the next and most important practice.

Purpose of the Moment

'There is plenty of time for that, when I have made my fortune. Everyone is always telling me that I have my whole life ahead of me, after all, and even you, Master, have always taught me that it's my life!'

'And so it is.' replied the sage. 'And your first duty must be to express yourself in your own unique way by being yourself. But to do that you must seek to harness your life force to the full, and that cannot be achieved without knowledge of your unique purpose.'

'I do hear what you say and I respect your wisdom, but try as I might I have no answer to that which I am do to. I cannot waste my life waiting to know what it could be. I'm going to seek my fortune first so I can then live my life to the full. Come with me and we'll both seek our fortunes together.'

'Now is my time for knowledge,' replied the sage and watched as student Cheng marched off into the distance. It was some ten years before they met again.

'How so,' shouted Cheng, 'what brings a revered sage so far from home?'

'Now it is my time for life so I am travelling and teaching for a while. What fortune shines on you?'

'I have good employment,' Cheng replied, 'and a wife with three little ones, although they are not with me. But soon things will be different; it's just a matter of time.'

Ten years later Cheng meets his former tutor at The Dragon Festival.

'Another world we meet, what brings you to this province?' Cheng asked. 'For my part I am very close to something important.'

'Now is my time for power,' replied The Grand Master. This province has been given to me to rule over for a while.'

'But you are a seeker of knowledge and a teacher, this is so different to what you have always done,' said the startled Cheng.

'Not so at all, it is the next stepping stone in the river of my life's purpose. My attention has been on one stone at a time, not on the river flowing by. That I cannot stop and would not want to for it is the bringer of the opportunities that allow me to express my purpose. I follow each of my inclinations at a time, being assured of the stability of each stone before proceeding. In this way my direction is certain.'

A further ten years later the two meet while meditating in The Garden of Contemplation.

'You look well, Old Master,' said Cheng. 'The years have served you better than the ones that have served me in this life. My life seems empty with lack of meaning. I have come here to pray for direction'.

'Now is my time for contentment and peace, and it warms my heart to see you again,' answered the old sage. 'Prior to this, my time has served me well in respect of happiness of the heart. My initial inclination for knowledge put me in the right direction and every moment of my life I have sought to be ready to follow future inclinations at the right time.'

'It would seem that when a man intently and moment by moment is working on fulfilling his potential, he is expressing his purpose,' replied Cheng. 'The difference between us would appear to be that while I wanted to live my life to the full, you were actually doing so. What I believed was a future event was not at all.'

'Just so,' said the old sage, 'but even now we have a purpose to fulfil, because our rivers are still flowing. New water is as refreshing as when Youth meets Experience. It can never be too late to fulfil your purpose. It is a matter of letting go of what you believe is your security. For there is no security, there are only opportunities. Follow your heart and they will come to you.'

🕉 Every living being has a purpose, and it is the knowledge of that purpose that allows us to manifest the opportunities in the right place at the right time. Conversely, without knowledge of our specific purpose too many of life's opportunities pass by unnoticed.

🕉 In our modern world fortunes are regularly spent on changing and improving methodologies, yet the majority of businesses continue to last less than one generation, and the majority of working people retire disillusioned, unfulfilled. Usually their enormous energy and potential is misdirected. Having an external objective is not the same as living a purpose that is internally driven.

🕉 Striving is futile if those energies available for our growth are working against us. When we are uncertain of our purpose we will be unable to recognise the direction that is right for us. Moreover, our destination is pointless, if we are unable to recognise it when we arrive. When we are not in command of our own direction we will be distracted and go elsewhere. Our directions and arrivals relate to the processes and results we experience in our lives.

✶ Whatever our purpose, it can be understood by studying the six inclinations everyone has hidden within the depths of their heart. Being absorbed in the way of the world, many do not take the time to decide what that purpose is, but at the same time, there is a continual inclination towards it. These inclinations are as follows.

Desire of knowledge

✶ Every child wants to know the reason 'why?' In time, the adult comes to believe that work to earn one's bread and butter is the natural successor to education. We learn to get by and later strive in our work to get on until, without ever a moment to gain it, the hunger for knowledge is gone and the mind becomes blunted. Others, with time seek novelty, thinking that to learn means to get to know something new. Few see that in every simple idea is a revelation which will teach them more and more when they put their minds to it. Continuing to gain knowledge, knowing yourself and what motivates you, should be a part of daily life. In this way you are attracted to what is right for you to do.

Love of Life

✌ This is as important to human beings, as it is to every little insect that tries to escape your touch. However difficult and unhappy their life, every being wishes to live. Perhaps in the sadness of the moment a person might choose to commit suicide, but if he or she were in their normal state of mind they would not think of leaving the world. Not necessarily because the world is dear to them, but because it is their natural inclination to survive.

Gaining of Power

✌ In any situation power is sought because nature seems to sweep everything away that has no strength. The mistake we make is in the areas we choose to seek our strength. Power and control gained over people and things can only remain limited. History illustrates how even the most powerful nations, built over hundreds of years, can be crushed in a very short time; individuals, who seem to be all-powerful, can be brought to their knees in an unforeseen moment. The real power we should be seeking is power over ourselves.

Pursuit of Happiness

✌ This is at the very heart of Man, although he seldom looks for it there. It is sought in leisure and pleasure, anything that will bring momentary happiness. The reality is that only virtue can bring real happiness. Anything that is transitory or which ultimately leads to unhappiness cannot be true happiness. Goodness leads to happiness. What is good is good, because it gives happiness, and if it does not do so, it cannot be good, or right, or of virtue. Whenever Man has found virtue in unhappiness he has been mistaken; whenever he was wrong he was unhappy. Happiness is the very being of mind, and at any one moment Man knows how to question any source of unhappiness; though seldom seeks the answer within.

Attainment of Peace

⅄ You do not attain peace through rest, comfort or solitude. It is an art which is brought about when who we are and what we do is in harmony with our true-self. It is natural to experience peace, but life in our world is far from that. Animals and birds experience peace but Man is the robber of his own peace. From seeking security outside of ourselves, either through constant acquisition, our position, or the stance we adopt; to our continual comparison with how successful we consider ourselves to be over others, rather than seeking self-reliance and co-operation, we have created an artificial life far removed from that which nature intended for us. The art of discovering peace is not in making outside conditions better for us. It is in seeking it within ourselves.

Having Purpose

✗ At some stage in their life everyone asks themselves: 'Why am I here and what am I to accomplish in life?' It is a fact that however discontented and restless someone may be, the moment they have purpose to their life a light goes on inside them. They may not be able to accomplish it but knowing it provides all the inspiration, strength, hope and vigour they need to pursue it.

✗ One person with purpose will have greater power than a hundred working dawn 'til dusk not knowing their purpose. Out of one hundred people, ninety-nine will be discontented with the work they are doing. Either it is their life's condition that has placed them there, or it is because they have to work to live, or because they believe that they need to acquire the things that working makes affordable. By the time they have gathered what they need, the desire of wanting it has gone.

✗ Having purpose determines our sense of right or wrong, good or bad. For example, one person whose vocation is to write plays and another whose vocation is to practice medicine, have their examinations before them. There is a play advertised which prompts them both to feel, 'I want to go and see it.' The medical student thinks, 'I should really study, but this is a good play and I must see it.' The playwright thinks, 'To go and see this play might be beneficial.' Both act in the same way, seeing the same play, but one loses the sense of study and the other is inspired.

✹ If we do not know what part we are to play in the symphony of life, we will not be able to produce the music that is so necessary for our personal satisfaction. When we are out of rhythm with the notes available to us, it is difficult to get back in tune.

What have we done today?

✹ Living, trusting, accepting and being in harmony with our purpose are the keys for ensuring we are in the right place at the right time. The secret is knowing that the application of these keys work. The sea turtle will carry her eggs, once fertilised, for up to four years, knowing that the time will come when she arrives at the right place, to lay them. Yet how many offspring survive is still beyond her control.

✹ When Man thinks only about what he wants to achieve at a later date, he fails to live his purpose each moment. Like the turtle, many of us may carry our fertilised ideas and potential around for years, waiting for the right time and place to hatch them. The trouble is that the inner shell we have built up over our life prevents us from recognising when and where that time and place is. We either convince ourselves that we have missed out already, or that we can do whatever it is at some time in the future. It is vitally important that each of us begins to believe in ourselves.

✹ Using our present effectively, becoming conscious of knowing what is right for us and what we are about, builds that belief. If we let go of debilitating ties to the past, such as grievances and failures, and cease to feel concern as to what may or may not happen to us, we can focus all our energy on positioning us in the right place at the right time.

We shall do so much in the years to come,
But what have we done today?
We shall give our gold in a princely sum,
But what did we give today?
We shall lift the heart and dry the tear,
We shall plant a hope in the place of fear,
We shall speak the words of love and cheer,
But what did we give today?

We shall be so kind in the afterwhile,
But what have we been today?
We shall bring each lonely life a smile,
But what have we brought today?
We shall give to truth a grander birth,
And to steadfast faith a deeper worth,
We shall feed the hungering souls of earth,
But whom have we fed today?

We shall reap such joys in the by and by,
But what have we sown today?
We shall build us mansions in the sky,
But what have we built today?
'Tis sweet in idle dreams to bask,
But here and now do we do our task?
Yes, this is the thing our souls must ask,
'What have we done today?' Anon

Epilogue

'Three weeks on the road and all that greets me are smouldering ashes,' sighed the Merchant-Sage, Ni.

'What was it that you expected,' said a voice behind him. 'With all the provinces in such chaos! Where have you been?'

Turning round the merchant saw a young man in a bedraggled state, his face stained with blackened smoke and blood. Getting down from his horse Ni said. 'I had hoped that I would arrive before the Emperor Ch'in's outrages had reached this outpost. But, I see that I am too late. Has all been lost?'

'If you are a former graduate of this Academy, as I suspect you are,' said the man, 'you would be wise to take care. For they are imprisoning all who are followers of the ways of the ancients.'

'My ancestor, the renowned Merchant Ni, was the grand-nephew of the founding Patriarch, Yen Tzu. Our House is loyal to the philosophy he and his followers taught. And you—,' Ni once more surveyed the man before him, '—what part have you played to be in such a sorry state?'

'I, too, came here for a similar purpose, but alas I was also too late. My name is Lu, of the House of Chou, whose founding father was also a pupil of Yen Tzu. My young heart and legs were sent by my Uncle in an attempt to rescue what parchments I could. But all was already aflame when I arrived this morning. It must have burned all night. I have fallen many times and scorched myself in my frantic search, but to no avail.'

The two paused in silence as they surveyed the ruins around them. As they did so, their eyes rested on the main gate keystone that now stood alone, unaccompanied by its former walls. The charred words were still clear to see.

'So, not all is lost,' said Lu.

'Indeed, none of it can ever be lost,' added Ni, as together they read the stone's inscription.

Wisdom comes from one great Sage,
A true source for every age.
Mind, the door, Heart, the key,
Spirit guide, the path to be.
Listen within, Trust to feel,
Illusions vanish, Truth is real.

Review the way of self-mastery
through individual inner understanding with:

The Teachings of Billionaire Yen Tzu

Volume I